Paw ɼ rint

The Journal of Mirk, a Sheepdog Aged 6½ Years,
and His New Owner

Jean Tyers

Pen Press

First published in Great Britain by Pen Press

All paper used in the printing of this book has been made from wood grown in managed, sustainable forests.

ISBN13: 978-1-78003-730-1

Printed and bound in the UK
Pen Press is an imprint of
Indepenpress Publishing Limited
25 Eastern Place
Brighton
BN2 1GJ

A catalogue record of this book is available from the British Library

Cover design by Jacqueline Abromeit
Illustrations © Kathryn Brame

To my daughters, Louise and Emily

Acknowledgements

To acknowledge everyone who has influenced, supported, encouraged and loved us through this five-year process would have meant another chapter, so briefly:

To Louise and Emily, both of whom encouraged me to bring Mirk home, as did Yvonne Robson. I am grateful to Michael Carter who painstakingly typed out my handwritten copy and to Gillian Johnson for printing the manuscript. Dawn Shearsmith for her friendship and work on the text, and to Jean Braidwood, who, as my friend and proofreader, not only meticulously highlighted corrections but also typed them. Claire Spinks, editor, together with the team at Indepenpress. To Kathryn Brame, illustrator, for all her hard work and friendship. To all those who supplied me with photos to use in the book, especially Colin Forster, Elaine Craig and Louise Maddison.

Last but not least, to all my family and friends who have loved Mirk and believed in me, especially Ann and Terry Peate, who 'adopted' Mirk for walks and sleepovers.

Although this is a true story, some names have been changed throughout to protect the privacy of the individuals concerned.

Contents

Prologue

Without Mirk there would not be a book. Without the book there would not have been the opportunity to think about my faith in this way, and what an important part Mirk has played in all of this.

Having a Christian faith (my commitment to become a Christian was made at one of my lowest points of my life – my divorce) has certainly been the one steady factor in my life, over the last 35 years. My faith has been stretched and strengthened throughout this time. I had started a three-year social work course at the then Newcastle Polytechnic following my divorce, but during my second term became ill with inflammation of the heart muscle, caused by a viral infection. I rejoined the course after Easter but failed an exam, and was advised by my tutor to take a year off and to rejoin the course the following year, 1982; I was distraught. The large Victorian terraced house in Darlington had been sold, and I, together with my two daughters, Louise and Emily, had moved to a tiny flat in Durham. Now my grant had ceased and the only money to pay the mortgage, bills and food was the small allowance from Pete, my ex-husband, which left very little for days out and the car. Through prayer and support from St Nicholas Church in Durham, we just managed until the following year when I resumed my course. Qualifying in 1984, I took a job as a social worker with the Social Services Department in Chester-le-Street, as my final placement had been in the probation office there, which I had loved. In January 1985, I was appointed as a probation officer and worked in a town south of the county. By praying each morning, either in the shower or on the forty-minute journey to work, I put God firmly in the driving seat!

During my girls' teenage years, Emily began to have myoclonic jerks, where her arms had involuntary movements. If she had a cup or glass in her hand at the time, the contents (and the glass) would be thrown across the room. Then, one November morning in 1988, she had a seizure. She was in the bathroom, and I rushed to find her unconscious on the floor. Louise remained in her bedroom. I panicked and asked Louise to go for Marion, a neighbour. This was just the beginning: these episodes began to occur every ten days or so, until she was admitted to hospital following three seizures in less than 12 hours. Trying to stay calm, while reassuring Louise and explaining her condition to Emily was a very draining experience. I could not help but question – where was my God now?

Our friends Maureen and Richard, who had holidays in Ennerdale every June, asked Emily to go with them the following month with their two children, Helen and Peter. This was a very welcome break for me too; a break from lying awake each night listening for alarming sounds coming from Emily's bedroom that might indicate she was having another seizure. I realised that I couldn't go on like this. If this was how Emily was to be, then I needed to cope better. This came as a revelation to me one evening, when sitting with my good friend Ruth in my kitchen. I was upset and saying that I couldn't cope with all of this. She looked at me, and said:

"Well, do you have a choice?"

I was shocked. No, I didn't have a choice. This was my life and I just had to get on with it. From then on, I started to discipline myself by not thinking too much about the future, but just living each day as it came. Understandably, this was easier to say than do. Of course, I was terribly concerned about both the girls, more so Emily, but worry did not resolve anything.

At this time, Pete, their dad, had remarried, and the girls spent alternate weekends in Darlington with him, also visiting their grandparents. I really missed them. On their return, Sunday evening would normally bring with it bad behaviour! Going to and belonging to St Nicholas Church meant that I had some very good support and made friends. Prayer became an important part of planning and organising my day. I needed Him to walk with me to manage all that I needed to accomplish as my work was as demanding as ever.

In December, 1988, I moved to a remand centre and became responsible for two wings and a hospital ward of female prisoners. The women here were usually on remand for the most serious of crimes: murder, arson and violence. Some had taken the lives of their babies or children; others had killed their partners or husbands following years of abuse of various kinds. Many injured themselves. In the 80s and early 90s strip cells were still common, but at least I was able to sit on their mattresses on the floor with them and listen to their stories.

So where was God in all of this? This was perhaps the most challenging work. Trying to practise being in the presence of God took time, patience, prayer and space. Not easy when the girls needed attention and help with homework. (By the time Louise was eleven, this was beyond me!) Then there were the animals to feed and care for: at least two cats, and often the rabbits who loved being outside during the day. Not much time left for socialising.

The girls managed GCSEs and A Levels. Emily slept through most of her last two years but managed to stay awake for her theatre trips. I'll never forget *King Lear* at Newcastle's Theatre Royal, sitting in the gods for hours. By the time we left, I'd almost forgotten who I was!

Emily had some very supportive friends who knew exactly how to manage her epilepsy, so in this I saw that God was looking out for her. While she wasn't healed, she was having a happy two years with the Lord walking alongside her – wasn't that enough? One bleak Tuesday, driving home from work, I was suddenly hit from behind. I was second in a four-car shunt! Days earlier, Emily had had a seizure, and a day later, Louise had one too. Good friends, Christian and non-Christian, sustained me – found me the right car repairers with a courtesy car, and had the girls and me for supper. What more did I need?

***

Five years on, after having been given a Butler Trust award in March 1993 at the Holyrood Palace where I was presented to HRH The Princess Royal, I transferred to HMP Durham for a further two years. I covered the Segregation Unit and worked with men who had also been deeply scarred by traumatic childhood experiences. While the general public may see them as 'monsters', I saw them as vulnerable, hurting adults lost in a world of rejection, and being further abused by a system that neither cared nor understood, but by its very nature perpetuated the abuse. That is no excuse for their behaviour, of course, but a possible explanation. They are hurting so much, enough for many to attempt to take their own lives, sometimes succeeding.

The highlight of the month was when I organised and supervised children's visits. These were for low-risk prisoners, often in trusted working positions, both inside and outside the prison. The children would be collected from the visitors centre with the other parent or carer and taken to the chapel where the visits took place. There were toys, games and a host of activities for the men and their young children – here was a space where they could spend a couple of hours enjoying time with each other. One three-year-old was happy and content just to sit with her dad and feel his face, perhaps unable to believe he was real. On leaving one day, a six-year-old who had spotted the scaffolding on A-Wing, remarked, "My Dad used to work here." So what were the children told I wondered?

I pursued the idea of helping children come to terms with their separation and later, together with a prison officer, ran a group initially for the men on the visits. The group, which looked at the "How To Be A Better Parent In Prison" course, covered subjects like what the children were told, by whom, and why the children had been left without a parent. The course also helped these fathers to understand the importance of being truthful to their children, as well as how to support and listen to their wives and partners or other family members, many of whom were struggling alone with the issues of benefits and housing, as well as caring for their children.

Conferences and presentations followed, and the men themselves were challenged but welcomed the often thought-provoking situations these opportunities presented. God was certainly present on Tuesday mornings!

The visits and courses were, of course, all held in the chapel.

Time with the Family Court Welfare Team (later CAFCASS) came to an end in 1999 when my sister Anne learned that she was terminally ill. Just eleven weeks later, at the age of 56, she died. I was angry at Anne for not having any treatment, and at God for not healing her. She was such a great loss to all of us; she had been at the centre of the family. Anne was the button, the Velcro, the zip and the pin which held everything and everyone together – without her, we would all fall apart.

It had been Anne who introduced me to the idea of frequenting coffee shops when we shopped in Nottingham in the 70s. The first place I remember visiting with her was Ziggi's. When we went further afield, to houses and gardens and the like, it was always refreshing to stop for a while to chat about the place and learn some snippet of information from Anne that I did not know. All the better over a cup of coffee and a piece of shortbread. As a social historian, it was fascinating to listen to her and to share her enthusiasm for knowledge of how the people of the house lived, worked and socialised. Often the servants would marry the groom, gardener or gamekeeper, then remain close by. To see their shopping lists, recipes and other such items was intriguing and opened up all kinds of thoughts to the imagination.

Anne's death somehow made sense years later when, in February 2001, her youngest son Joe experienced the birth and death of baby George, his first child. Both Joe and his wife Ali were distraught and Emily and I stayed with them for a while before the service and visited baby George in the Chapel of Rest. He was beautiful. Had he gone to be with Anne?

Two months after Anne's death, my mum had a fall and broke her hip. She was in hospital for some time, during which she had a hip replacement. She was 88 years old. As she would be unable to return to her flat, it was time to consider bringing Mum to Durham. Her short-term memory loss was also becoming worse. Some days she would not remember that Anne had died. So how did I cope? Overwhelmed at times with losing Anne, I felt lost and alone. Only through the prayers and support of my friends did I survive one day at a time. Often I was too sad to pray, and why would I pray anyway? Anne had gone, and left a hole in my heart, a hole so big that I still felt empty. But then I tried to remember all the good times.

Even so, what would I pray for anyway? Some days I did not know how to survive the next five minutes, let alone the rest of the day or week. The only way was to live totally in the present moment, not only by just dealing with each problem to be solved as it came along but also by being fully aware of whatever I was doing. Where would Mum live? She was later moved from the Queen's Medical Centre, Nottingham to a rehabilitation hospital, which was easier for visiting. Emily, by now, was back home with me and a great support. After visiting Mum on Fridays we would drive to the nearby multiplex cinema and watch a film for some escapism and a little light relief.

In June, Mum came to Durham by ambulance, and enjoyed her last three years being visited by myself and the girls, as well as her nephews and also a friend of mine, Maureen, whom she had met on many previous visits to Durham. Mum died 6 June 2002.

***

When I look at Mirk I see a very trusting dog. As we began to spend our time together, we learnt about each other's ways. I thought how my trust in God had grown and developed over the last few years. Isn't my relationship with Mirk a bit like how mine should be with God? It has to start somewhere, after all. When I first asked Mirk to jump into the car boot and drove off with him for a new life, my commitment had begun. I promised that I would love, feed, exercise, play and share my life with him. Isn't that what God promises us too? To provide for all our needs. To never leave us, but to walk alongside us in all our pain and suffering. That is what I will do for Mirk, and he, for me.

I watch him as he sits at my feet, resting, a bit like Mary, and when I move, he follows me from room to room. Yes, we have some rules and discipline. I feed Mirk the right amount of good food so that he stays fit and well and always enjoys his walks. Oh, how I wish I could discipline myself as well! Mirk lives only in the present, always ready to obey, even though he does not know what I will ask of him. A step of faith into the unknown. As we grow closer together, we enjoy each other more. Just living in the present, and in the presence of God. Enough.

Paws for Thought

There was a time in my life when everything seemed straightforward. For thousands of years, dogs like me were bred for one specific purpose – to herd sheep or other livestock. I had a happy puppyhood with my brothers and sisters, being trained by Elaine to a very high standard for the role we were to undertake.

One day, it was time for me to begin my work with a new farmer, so I left with Jack and happily followed him everywhere. I knew my place and if he moved, I moved, always ready to obey. We became inseparable.

After many long, happy years herding his sheep, he suddenly disappeared. I didn't know why or where. I felt uneasy. People came and spoke in hushed voices, 'what will become of Mirk?' I seemed to go from one farm to another with no one wanting me. I was shut in a shed, where I felt afraid and very sad with nothing to do. Then one day, I heard a voice that I recognised. It was Elaine, the farmer who had trained me. She spoke quietly to me, and although she left me, a few days later she returned. I went back to her farm, where I was reunited with my half-brother Kirk, who was born the previous year. As I was not needed on the farm, Elaine tried to find me a new owner.

So this is where we begin....

Wanted

Good home for a 6½-year-old collie, Mirk

TEL: 09750 42**50 - Elaine

Introduction

The idea to have a dog had been in my mind for many years. On several occasions I had enjoyed walking in the company of friends and their dogs, but I had no fixed ideas about breed, just that it would be a medium to large dog. However, I had been brought up with cats, and was now working full time, so this never came to fruition.

It was Emily, my youngest daughter, who found Sam.

"A large ginger tom," I had said to her on deciding that we needed another cat, a friend for Moses. Emily set about the task instantly and began scanning the newsagent's windows on the local estate. We answered an advert a few days later for a ginger and white tomcat living close by. We duly called the number and arranged to visit.

It was on a Tuesday evening at 7.30pm, and Charlotte, Emily's best friend, came with us. We went into the lounge and there he was, gingerly walking along the arm of the sofa. He had been given a home here following the death of the couple's previous cat, but they also had a very large German Shepherd dog who did not take to his new 'pal'. Hence, a new owner was required. In turn, we picked him up and cuddled him before we took him home with us.

He immediately felt very much at home sitting on a shoulder. He would climb up there and lie along the back of your neck, across your shoulders, and there he would quite happily remain for ages, purring loudly. We renamed him Sampson – strong! He had lovely soft fur, a thick coat, and his face displayed an inverted V which was all white, reaching to a point above his nose and between his eyes; a very handsome fellow indeed. Over the years he became so dependable. During this time, our other cat Moses died, and Emily left home for college, after which there had been just the two of us for many years. He became my favourite of all the cats I had owned.

In January 2007, Sam, now aged 13½, suddenly became ill and had difficulty breathing. A visit to a veterinary clinic some miles away – it was a Saturday evening – revealed that he had fluid on his lungs which would require draining and an overnight stay in an oxygen tent to help him breathe. The next morning, he greeted me and appeared to be much better, but I was told that he would need medication for the rest of his life, and in any event, his life expectancy would be only a matter of months.

Making a decision about Sam was difficult for me. He was a terror when it came to taking pills, and days later I would find them in various parts of the house. Having pretended to swallow the pill while really keeping it hidden away in his mouth, he would later deposit it elsewhere! If the same thing were to happen again and his lungs filled with fluid whilst he was outside then he could collapse and I might never be able to find him. I felt that I could not put Sam through this, and as a 'hunter' he would have hated to be kept indoors all the time. I said goodbye to Sam, and held him one last time, told him I loved him, and thanked him for coming into my life and giving me, and my friends and family, so much love and affection. I stayed with him until he had taken his last breath. It was a very, very sad day, and I vowed that he would be my very last cat ever.

***

At the beginning of 2008 I retired from my profession as a probation officer. I began to plan and filled the rest of the year by visiting family and friends, as well as booking a couple of working holidays with the National Trust and the RSPB. As I was already doing voluntary conservation work with the local coast and countryside group, it seemed the obvious way to go.

So in August I was off to Rathlin Island, just off the north coast of Northern Ireland, for two weeks with the RSPB, showing visitors the various sea birds nesting there. I had planned to spend a night in Stranraer in order to take the first ferry to Belfast the following morning. Driving through Dumfries and Galloway I stopped en route at Bellymack Farm, where each day the owners, Ann and Pam, feed the red kites from a large wooden table in a field. I had visited there before and loved to watch these magnificent birds of prey interact with each other, swooping and flying effortlessly, allowing the thermal air currents to dictate their movements. These birds could be watched from the car park or to the side of the farm buildings from an RSPB bird hide. Whilst I was there, one of the owners, Ann, came over and as we chatted she happened to mention that a local collie needed a home, and pointed to a small piece of paper pinned on the notice board: "Wanted – good home for a 6½-year-old collie, Mirk TEL 09750 42**50 – Elaine."

This sounded like a real possibility – a dog of my own! I was very interested and took all the relevant details, driving away in a happy daze. What was I doing? I gave myself a good talking to: *are you insane? At last you have the freedom to go where you want, when you want, with no restrictions and you're thinking of taking on a dog? You have no idea what it entails!* Pushing these negative thoughts aside, I stopped for coffee and called the farmer. We arranged that I would call at the farm in two weeks' time, on Sunday 1 September, at 10am, to meet both her and Mirk. She later texted me the name of her farm which I located on an OS map, up on the hillside, high above two hamlets on the outskirts of Gatehouse of Fleet.

During the next couple of weeks I spoke to a friend and to both my girls to obtain reassurance and support for the imminent arrival of a new family member. Was I making the right decision for both of us? If I'm really honest, I'd already decided that Mirk would be going home with me – if he was still available. I prayed very hard that evening and thought of little else.

***

Rathlin Island marks the most northerly point in Northern Ireland. It lies six miles north of County Antrim and 15.5 miles south of the Mull of Kintyre. The population of almost 100 human residents is greatly increased during the spring and summer months when visitors to the Seabird Centre, located at the westerly lighthouse, are rewarded with eye-level views of a great variety of sea birds. By the time I arrived in mid-August, only the fulmars and kittiwakes remained; the puffins, guillemots, razorbills and shags all having left as soon as their breeding season was over and their offspring had fledged.

As the island is only about four miles long, the best way to explore it is on foot or bike. These are quiet lanes and the only road leads from the harbour to the three lighthouses, one at each corner. The sea around the island has a wealth of marine life and, with 70-metre-high cliffs, there are plenty of clifftop habitats for all manner of birds and wildlife. Dolphins, harbour porpoises and grey seals are often seen from the ferry, and on the cliffs, the birds can be seen bickering over their nest sites, incubating eggs, feeding the chicks, and flying on and off the island to hunt for their next meal. It is interesting to see how the different birds arrange themselves on the different levels of the cliff; puffins in the burrows, razorbills choosing tucked-away crevices, and guillemots packed tightly together on the very narrow ledges. Gannets flying past and diving into the sea for fish, provided an entertaining hour for visitors one afternoon, their flying expertise equal to a Red Arrows' display!

The visitors to the island were a welcome distraction during the daytime and the evenings gave me time to think about Mirk. Would he take to living in a house? Would he like me? The doubts kept coming, but I decided that, despite all the "what ifs", I would rather live with the consequences and overcome any difficulties than not take the opportunity together with all the associated risks. So the decision was made, with all that this might entail.

At quiet times during the day, I made myself busy and learnt about other seabirds. The recently departed puffins, razorbills and guillemots were, by now, on their way over the Atlantic Ocean before returning again next spring. The visitors, however, continued arriving by ferry and were driven up to the lighthouse where a new visitors' centre was open. Here they could learn about the seabirds from the interpretation boards before descending the steep steps to the lighthouse.

Two weeks passed, during which we attended Sports Day, an annual community event. We participated not only in all manner of races but also in face painting and other fun events. We also manned an RSPB stall, set out to attract new members and to increase public awareness of the island and its birdlife. As volunteers, it was expected that we should participate fully in order to become part of the community and so we all immersed ourselves in island life. A day off each week enabled us to explore the Northern Ireland coastline, visiting Carrick-a-Rede, a rope bridge traditionally erected by salmon fishermen across a chasm 30 metres deep and 20 metres wide; an exhilarating experience!

The second week, Laura, a volunteer, joined us and it was good to meet up with her again. We had met the previous year on a National Trust working holiday at Strangford Lough and we had kept in touch. Laura had been at Durham University, after which she had moved to Newcastle where she now lived and worked. She came down to help with my first ever litter-pick on my adopted beach just weeks after we returned from Strangford Lough. She was great fun and later returned to Strangford for a further few months. It was good to have Laura around to bounce off ideas about becoming a dog owner.

On our last evening all the volunteers, together with Alison and Liam who are resident on the island and manage the project, went to the only hotel by the harbour where we enjoyed a meal and shared our thoughts about our time spent on the island. The following morning, Laura and I drove down to Belfast and there I left her as she was getting a lift to Dublin. I boarded the ferry, and spent the journey thinking about Mirk, wondering how different my life would be from now on, and praying that he would soon be mine.

Sunday, 1 September 2008 – the Homecoming

As I was driving from Stranraer to Gatehouse of Fleet, the rain came down in torrents. The car was packed with leftover food, wellingtons, jackets, a sleeping bag and clothing. It was past 10am when I arrived at the farm, having opened the gate and avoided the herd of cattle on the track. I was met by five barking dogs, followed by their owner, Elaine. The four border collies were her working dogs, and the German Shepherd a guard dog.

"Wow!" I exclaimed. "Which one is Mirk?"

"Oh, none of these," she replied. "Mirk's in the barn drying off after his walk."

I was led into the kitchen where I waited tentatively for Mirk to appear. I will never forget this meeting; Mirk came straight in and sat down in front of me, offering me his big right paw which he then placed upon my knee. I stroked him, thinking how big he was, and wondering if I would be able to handle him. I decided to keep my thoughts to myself.

I did notice, however, that Mirk avoided all eye contact by moving his gaze from side to side. Did he not trust me? Then again, why would he?

Apparently Mirk, having been bred locally, then went to be trained by Elaine from the age of 7 weeks before moving on. Mirk worked for several years before his farmer died. After that, Mirk's tail became sadder and sadder, but he was rescued in the nick of time by Elaine.

Elaine and I exchanged information, and she asked, "Where will he be sleeping?"

"Under the stairs," I replied.

"He won't be shut in, will he?"

"No, not at all." I explained that I never closed doors so Mirk would be able to go as he pleased. He would have access to my kitchen and lounge, a large room with patio doors, which overlooked the garden. I asked about his food, and she gave me enough to last until I was able to buy some. He had not received any inoculations, nor had he been wormed. In fact, all he had was what he stood up in – his tri-coloured brown, black and white coat, and his red collar!

Outside in the farmyard, we reorganised my belongings onto the back seat of the car, leaving the boot area completely clear for Mirk. We removed the parcel shelf and the car was ready. Mirk jumped in and sat there proudly, perhaps believing he was a very special dog. As Mirk did not have a lead, Elaine found a piece of green twine which was tied to his red collar and secured in the boot of the car.

All set, off we went. I watched through my rear view mirror as Mirk sat bolt upright, watching the farm disappear from view. Eventually, having reached the A75, we made haste to Durham as I needed to buy several items for Mirk, including some toys, bedding and a lead. As it was a Sunday, a local pet store would only be open until 4pm, so there was now some urgency as the time was ticking by. As I glanced into my rear view mirror, Mirk would be sitting up, looking out of the window as we passed field upon field of sheep. Mirk must have thought, 'What an adventure!' Or maybe he didn't think at all. Or maybe he just enjoyed being in the moment without the concerns of 'When will I be fed? Or go for a walk?' Little did I realise at that point, just how much I was to learn about trust over the coming weeks and months.

Now on the A69, heading towards Newcastle, I realised that I needed to stop for a coffee and to eat and use the facilities. I found a farm shop, and first of all got Mirk out of the car and walked him round the car park to a quiet area in the corner by some trees. He, too, used the facilities, and all the time in my head I was making a mental shopping list of other items which I would need to buy. Back in the car for Mirk! I left the windows open a little for him and sped off to see to my own needs! I drank a cup of coffee in record time. There was no time to look around the shop; although I did need some food, that could wait. At 3.40pm I drove into the parking area of the pet store in Durham and found an assistant to help me with some purchases: a new blue collar and lead, some toys, a bed, food, treats, poo bags and a grooming comb. And off I went some £100 lighter!

The last stretch of the journey found me thinking about what I needed to do on reaching home. I also thought that Mirk would need some boundaries; where should I allow him to go and what would be acceptable behaviour? I recalled that some fifteen years earlier, following the death of her dad, Emi, my youngest daughter, had returned home from college and remained with me for a couple of years. During this time she had looked after a guide dog puppy who ate anything and everything, including toothpaste! But a puppy was very different from a 6½-year-old Border collie. I remembered then what I had forgotten to ask about – his commands! Did I need a whistle? And a host of other questions. Too late, I thought, as I parked the car. Should I take Mirk in first or last? It would take me ages to unpack the car. There was an open grassy area between my house and the car park, so I was some distance away. I decided to take in my belongings, remove my bike, which I had left in the hallway, into the back garden, then bring Mirk in last. He watched intelligently every time I took things from the car, deposited them, and returned again and again and again.

Finally, it was Mirk's turn. He jumped down and I held him firmly by the green twine which joined us together. He sniffed and I took him alongside the outer edge of the grass area near a fence which adjoined a field. On reaching the front door, Mirk hesitated. He continued to stand his ground until I led the way and he duly followed. So that was it – a truly well-mannered dog! I removed his make-shift green lead and rolled it up. I walked into the large kitchen-dining area, talking to him all the time in a calm voice to reassure him that these were the places he could go. I unpacked his new bowls, gave them a quick wash and filled one with fresh cold water. By now it was well after five o'clock, so I decided that he must be hungry and proceeded to measure out by hand what I thought would be the right amount of food, given that I had no idea of his weight. While he ate, I made up his bed in the corner with a large basket and soft blanket and a towel. Mirk refused to go in, walking up to it, then away again. He obviously didn't like the basket, so I removed it, placing the other items on the floor. He immediately sat down, circling twice on his bed before lying down and falling fast asleep, curled up like a cat. Now it was my turn, so I unpacked some leftover food and hastily cooked a meal. Mirk's bed was directly opposite the kitchen door, which was never shut, and he didn't stir despite my comings and goings between the kitchen and the lounge. A couple of hours later when I was in the lounge watching the television, Mirk awoke and came to find me. I made a fuss of him, stroked his brown, black and white coat and fondled his ears. I told him that this was now his home, and that he was very welcome, and that over the coming days, months and years each of us would be an important part of the other's life. I sat on the floor to be at his level and cupped his tri-coloured face in my hands and spoke softly to him. I counted the beauty spots just above his nose, randomly placed as if splattered by an artist's paintbrush. I reflected on the V-shaped white area tapering between his eyes and onto his forehead. Slightly above and to the side of each eye, his brown eyebrows moved up and down as he moved his eyes from side to side. His paws were large, all white with long claws. I began to think about ringing the vet in the morning to arrange a health check and to discuss Mirk's general welfare.

As he curled up on a Jacob sheepskin rug, blissfully unaware of my concerns to do the right thing by him, I told him that we were now in this together, that I may not always get it right but that we would help each other. I would play with him and try not to be overprotective. I would walk, groom, feed and love him. He took a deep sigh, then relaxed. I glanced around the room, which looked very different from when I left over two weeks ago. Yes, this was for real: I was now the proud, responsible owner of a very handsome and beautiful Border collie, and from now on, both our lives would change forever. There was no going back. This was my commitment to Mirk.

Early Days

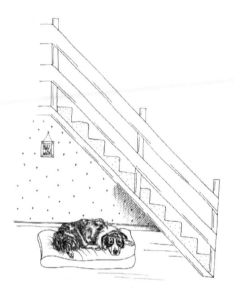

I awoke the next morning at 6.15am. I lay there, collecting my thoughts. Oh yes, Mirk's downstairs, I need to walk him! I listened but could not hear a sound. I pulled on a pair of jogging pants, went to the bathroom, grabbed a T-shirt and went downstairs. Mirk greeted me with a wagging tail. I put on my boots, attached his new lead to his new blue collar, and off we went as Mirk was already dressed in his brown, black and white coat. Not knowing, or having any plan as to how far to go or how long this would take, we set off, poo bags in my pocket. Mirk pulled very hard and I quickly realised he was definitely not used to being on a lead! I pulled him back, stopped and waited, then set off again.

The same happened, so I repeated the previous exercise! Eventually, we were past the houses and walking along the public bridleway separating HMP Frankland from the housing estate, and round by Low Newton Nature Reserve. Mirk was still pulling furiously, so much so that I began jogging! After around half an hour or so we returned home by the same route. Mirk had a very small amount of food. I showered, had breakfast, then embarked upon countless telephone calls to announce the safe arrival of Mirk. Not much of a surprise then for those who knew me!

I recalled how one Easter Monday in the late 80s, I took the girls to a large garden centre for some garden plants. It was meant to be a short trip as in the afternoon we would go walking. Not so! This particular garden centre had a pet section, whereupon I spied a very forlorn-looking rabbit with long ears. She was a strawberry blonde! The girls had kept rabbits previously, and we still had the hutch that their dad had made, which was in good condition. I looked at the small array of plants in my basket and thought I'd better put them back; no time to plant these if rabbit comes home with us! The girls were excited; we called her Abbie – paid £5 and left. So not so surprising that now the girls were saying, 'No, not again... Off she goes on a voluntary working holiday, and comes home with a Border collie. Whatever next!'

And so an appointment was made for Mirk for that afternoon at the vet's for a general health check, and to discuss his requirements in terms of healthcare. I took along his pedigree document, given to me by Elaine, and my credit card. Mirk was weighed; he was 31kg which was about right for his breed, but I was advised not to allow him to gain any more weight. His ears, eyes, teeth and coat were examined and happily, there was no indication of anything untoward. An appointment was made for the following Wednesday for Mirk to spend most of the day there to be castrated, micro-chipped, and to have his teeth cleaned. He was also started on a course of inoculations with follow-up appointments as required. In the waiting room there was a notice board with advertisements for various grooming services, trainers, dog walkers and pets for sale. I took down some details of the local agricultural college where they were looking for a variety of dog breeds to groom for the new intake of students. Throughout the whole visit, Mirk remained calm and showed a very placid nature. Whilst he wasn't eager to get on the scales or enter the consulting room, he nonetheless cooperated after being encouraged with treats. There was no jumping up, barking or any other anti-social behaviour. I was very proud of him!

Not knowing what commands he knew, I began with just the basics: sit, stand and lie down. Another command that I tried was to ask him to wait until I gave him the order to eat his food. He enjoyed his meal despite eating the same food, day in, day out; he always cleaned his bowl and was thankful.

***

In time our days became more structured. I thought that if I did the same each day, a routine would be established so that Mirk would come to know what to expect. So, on waking, my first priority was to walk him. Then he would quite happily lie on his bed for several hours while I attended to my own work in the house and garden. This gave us both our own space. At around midday, we would take a ball on a rope or a frisbee onto the front grass area where we would play for 20 minutes or so. It wasn't easy to keep Mirk's attention. He loved to just wander off and sniff around the entire area, checking out other dogs. He learned to run after anything I threw for him, but still could not get the hang of bringing them back for me to throw again. His favourite was a ball with shapes cut out where his treats could be placed. He would keep rolling it around to take the treats as they fell out, before walking away. If he heard a sound that he didn't like, Mirk would run to the open front door to take refuge. He had a strong dislike of motorbikes, reversing lorries, and gunshots. Car horns, electrical appliances and fireworks were also just too much for him.

Exploring the local nature reserve just half a mile from home was where Mirk enjoyed his freedom. From the road leading to HMP Frankland, a bridleway turned right, running alongside the prison. Here there would often be prison officers with their spaniels and German Shepherd dogs patrolling around the perimeter wall, looking for, and often finding, items that should not be there. Past the car park, the path continued before giving a choice of right or left at the top of the lane. The left path took a route passing two ponds where swans and other wildlife made their homes so, not wanting to disturb them, I did not take Mirk along there. Instead, we circled round to the right and walked until we met the path which took us down to a farm. Here there were fields of sheep, which Mirk liked. He stood and watched them from a distance, and some, if they were close enough, would stare back at him.

Down past Frankland Farm the path passed more fields which then joined another path. Turning left would be a circular route leading back, while turning right would take you into Durham City. This way led past Crook Hall, a beautiful thirteenth-century, Grade-1-listed medieval building where three eras of architecture exist alongside each other. The Medieval Hall was built around 1208; the Jacobean Mansion was added in 1671, and in 1720 the Georgian House was completed. This is family-owned now, by Keith and Maggie Bell, and the beautiful garden, once described by Alan Titchmarsh as "a tapestry of colourful blooms", is easily manageable as an afternoon stroll. It is worth lingering by the pond on a warm summer's day to watch the enormous dragonflies and damselflies. An excellent cream tea is served in the garden or courtyard, or inside if you wish. Well-behaved dogs are permitted in the grounds on leads but cannot go inside the house.

The woods around the Botanic Gardens were also a favourite of ours. Circular walks abound and all led back to the café and small shop. It was here that I would bring my mum before she died in 2002. Many happy hours were spent in the gardens, and a seat still marks the spot where Emily and I would bring her and where we drank tea and ate cherry scones. On one occasion, Richard, her eldest grandson, came by train from Nottingham specially to have lunch with her. Although Mirk was not allowed in the garden, he was allowed to sit in the shade by the entrance on the grass and enjoy a bowl of water.

The woods were home to all manner of birds and were very popular with dog walkers. The changing seasons brought changing smells, as the trees shed their leaves and the brown path turned to a golden yellow and brown carpet beneath our feet and paws! A flock of rare-breed sheep were in one of two fields and again, Mirk would go up to the gate to have a closer look. Nose to the ground, he would then trot off in search of more smells. If he went too far ahead, I only had to call him and he would wait until I'd almost caught him up, then he would be off again. By the time we reached the car park, Mirk would be on his lead. He had no road sense whatsoever, and why would he, having been brought up on farms in rural areas.

Mirk was placid, patient and gentle. It was difficult for anyone, even non-dog-owners, not to be drawn towards his well-structured, tri-coloured face and wagging tail. Everyone he met told him he was beautiful as they cupped his face in their hands. I would answer for him: "Do you mean me or my dog?" "Oh, your dog," came the reply. He seemed to have a way of allowing people to share their experiences of their dogs, and even more so with owners who had lost their dogs and were often still very sad. It was as if Mirk brought comfort just by allowing people to stroke and talk to him, helping them with their grieving process. In all, he was a very therapeutic dog. In fact, before leaving Durham, I contacted the Pets As Therapy organisation and Mirk was assessed and was deemed suitable to begin visits. Due to our move, however, I decided to wait until we were in Cockermouth, but this never materialised. The coordinator failed to respond to my messages – written, texts and verbal messages – all were ignored. Never mind, Mirk does his unofficial therapy around the towns and villages, on the fells and in the woods, anywhere that people meet him and want to tell him their stories. Perhaps you've met him?

Dogs are great levellers – keeping people grounded and in touch with the real world. There are no clocks in a dog's world, only time to eat, sleep, walk, play and be loved. Mirk treated everyone the same by giving unconditional love. There was no discrimination.

As Mirk had been bred and trained as a working sheepdog, he was not used to city living and all the roads, buses and trains. Gradually, I slowly introduced these to him. Firstly, we caught the local bus to the shopping centre where there was a pet store – fun for Mirk who would be given treats at the checkout – then walked back home as there were paths through the housing estate away from the road. The vet's surgery, cafés and visiting friends' houses all became familiar to him and he loved being around people just as much as other dogs. Some friends were amazed that I had a dog – after a lifetime of cats! And a working dog at that – "wow, how brave", some said. But I, in my naivety, refused to consider any downside or difficulties I might face, and certainly ignorance can be bliss in many ways. I guess if I had expressed all my fears, or worried about how problematic it may be, I might have passed up this opportunity and that would have been a big mistake – for both of us.

***

So Mirk gradually learned what was okay and what was not. I decided that he needed discipline but only where it was necessary to protect him and for him to know that I was now his mistress. My principles were largely based upon what I had disliked most about other dogs and what their owners allowed them to do. I was determined that Mirk would not eat my food, would not be allowed on the furniture, nor was he allowed upstairs. He made no attempt to do any of these; once he had been fed, he would rest for a while and paid no attention to my meal. After I had gone to bed he would lie at the foot of the stairs.

It was very frustrating for both of us to train Mirk to come when called and walk to heel. Before he was allowed off his lead, I needed to be sure that he would come back to me when I called him, and that he would stay safe and not be at risk from other dogs should any take a dislike to him. I would attach a very long lead to his blue collar and we would go onto the grassed area. I would ask him to sit, which he would do, then I would praise him, and tell him he was a clever/good boy. I would then ask him to 'stay' and walk away from him still holding the lead loosely, the idea being that I would turn to face him and call him and he would then trot towards me. Not so. When I turned to walk away, Mirk would immediately follow me. We tried it again, again and again.

How I envied the dog walkers that I saw with their dogs neatly trotting to heel, so close were they that they were almost in their shoes! Not having had Mirk as a puppy was both an advantage and a disadvantage. He was a mature dog who never jumped up and licked people. He was a very patient, tolerant dog. When we visited a friend's daughter, Amanda had acquired a Border Terrier named Bob for her partner, Neil. Bob would make a great fuss of Mirk. But Bob began to lose his eyesight over a period of time, and whenever he and Mirk were together, Bob would give Mirk lots of attention by placing his paws on Mirk's face and licking him. Mirk, as always, was very patient and when he had had enough, he would simply walk away.

It took a while for Mirk to engage with some of the toys that I had bought for him. He liked the ball on a rope and he would play tug with me, but I had to let him win every game. I was unsure if this was wise, but as he had the knack of sinking his teeth into the rope which I held, his mouth was perilously close to my fingers. He liked a larger ball that he could chase after if I threw or kicked it. He was not very good at bringing them back to me though. Mirk had a short attention span when he was playing and invariably would wander off the moment that he caught a whiff of something far more interesting. He would abandon play to investigate. However, by making playtime coincide with lunchtime, more or less, it meant that some neighbours would be returning home from work at the local prison. Mirk would greet them before resuming his game – that is, of course, if he could remember where he left his ball!

Like other dogs, Mirk loved his food. However, I stuck with the food that Mirk was used to. He had his main meal at around 5pm, and a small amount after his early morning walk. At lunchtime, after playing, he would enjoy a dental chew. Treats were only given as rewards, in moderation, and would be deducted from his daily allowance. He never tired of eating the same food, day in, day out. He still has the same food, only now the 'weight control' version! However, Mirk was always on the lookout for opportunities to obtain extras. If, for example, I inadvertently left his food bag slightly open, Mirk would try to open it further by poking his nose into the bag. I do not understand why some owners give their dogs their human food – especially the processed variety. I will not allow other people to give Mirk anything that I disapprove of, and if he is ever left with friends, I know that they respect my wishes and love Mirk too much to do anything different.

I often wondered if he ever missed his previous way of life, the freedom of the farm, and his life as a working dog – that herding instinct that would never leave him. Sometimes, as the days passed and we began to trust each other, he would look directly at me as if to say,

"Well, this life is fine, but where are your sheep?"

Knowing so little about his working life – together with Mirk being my first dog – it was a case of trial and error. It took several weeks before I could trust him on some walks off his lead. The evenings were our time to relax and he would wander into the lounge and take up his place on the Jacob sheep rug, quite obviously meant for him. I would groom him and tell him how happy I was to be a part of his life. He would roll onto his side, and often he appeared to be dreaming – of what, I wondered? But the big sigh as he lay there was proof of his contentment.

As I watched him I recalled many years ago, when I had prayed for a walking companion, someone to spend weekends and holidays with. I had an image of a younger guy, fun to be with, and also in want of a walking companion. Lo and behold, when attending an Alpha course at St Nicholas's Church, Durham, I met such a one, but Diana was female. Oh well, I thought, better than nothing! We enjoyed many years of walking in the Dales; Teesdale, Swaledale and several holidays in Southern Ireland and on the Isle of Skye. By the time of the foot-and-mouth outbreak in 2001, I had begun to spend more time swimming, and took a diploma in teaching swimming using the basic principles of the Alexander Technique. But alas, something was still missing. So I prayed again. Only this time I'd be more specific I thought, so I asked for a male walking companion, and He gave me Mirk! Was this God's idea of a joke? Well, at least, He has a sense of humour! And yes, I still do pray for a male walking companion – with two legs, not four!

Planning the Move – July 2008

Two months before Mirk appeared on the scene, I went to the Keswick Convention in July. When I'm in any town, I always like to look in estate agents' windows, dreaming of what I might be able to afford should I desire to move. At that moment in time, it would have been a one-bedroom apartment above a chippy! Well, add prayer to the situation, and anything is possible. After all, since my late teens, when a friend and I had travelled to the Lake District from Nottingham to climb and walk with a climbing club, I had always felt so sad to leave. We then both decided to move to the north-east and were able to transfer there for our respective jobs, and it all slotted into place. I recall happy memories of meeting my husband, Pete, in the Sun Inn at Coniston, and how, later, our eldest daughter Louise enjoyed her first holiday in Grasmere in a tiny cottage behind the Red Lion. Then, when Emily came along, we were fortunate to have friends in Darlington who loaned us their caravan on a site at Pooley Bridge for three consecutive years. As the girls were growing up, an escape to the Lakes was always our first choice. So it was no surprise then that one November day Mirk and I set off to stay at Nab Cottage near Rydal for a long weekend to check out property in the area. It made sense now, with Mirk, to relocate where there were walks in all corners and proverbially "more sheep than people". I guess he knew that this was something of an adventure, as his food, bedding, bowls and towels together with my bag were placed in the car. His first weekend break!

Arriving at Nab Cottage, at around 3pm, we were shown to our room along a corridor and up a wonky staircase. How quaint! I wondered if Thomas De Quincy thought the same when he was here in 1817. The room was comfortable enough; the double bed dominated the space, and the wardrobe with the long mirror on the door stood in a corner. The window seat was handy, as there was little surface space, and I could just fit into the en suite. Mirk seemed fascinated by the mirror; seeing his image reflected in the glass for the first time, he just sat in front of it, either staring at or, perhaps, admiring himself? I'm not sure which.

We hurried out and across the road turning left to the car park between Rydal Water and Grasmere. Mirk was eager for a walk, after only two brief stops on the way, and it wasn't long before we reached some trees through the wooded area and, going through a gate, we headed towards Grasmere. The wood was a delight for Mirk as he sniffed his way along, stopping at every tree to leave his mark. After half an hour or so, the light was beginning to fade, so we retraced our steps and headed back. Once, along the path leading to the car park, Mirk suddenly stopped in his tracks and looked to his right, to a clearing in the trees. There, stood a very handsome roe deer. For what appeared to be ages, nothing moved. Then, as suddenly as he appeared, he vanished, darting off in the direction of the water. It was an experience like this that reaffirmed my decision to move to the Lakes. We quickly returned to the cottage and after a meal, settled down to plan for tomorrow.

***

A good night's sleep and breakfast saw us on the move again, and we visited Ambleside, Grasmere and Keswick over the next three days. But alas, all these places seemed to be out of reach, not only because of the house prices, but also because there were employment and residence restrictions on the cheaper properties, in order to prevent people buying them but not living in them, which would not be good for the local economy. So we still enjoyed the area and made the most of its many walks, but we had to rule out these areas as a place to live. Not disheartened, we headed home to rethink – where could we try next?

With the map spread out on the pine kitchen table, I traced a line along the A66 with my finger. I really needed to be somewhere easily accessible, so I could quickly travel back to Durham, and also so that my friends and family could come and visit us. I decided that Penrith was too large for us, but just beyond Keswick, to the west, was the town of Cockermouth. I knew that this was where William Wordsworth was born, but I had never visited it. I had an idea that Louise might know more, so I called her to ask her opinion. She immediately said,

"Oh Mum, it's a lovely little town, you'll love it there." She went on to say that when she and a previous partner went up to the Caldbeck Fells and camped, they often visited the area. So with our next destination settled, I decided that Louise should accompany us on our next trip a few weeks later to explore Cockermouth.

I found a five-star B&B on the internet which was a dog-friendly establishment. I chose it not only for that reason, but also because the owners were called Jeanette and Andrew, and I had Christian friends of the same names. I booked this for three nights in December, just before Christmas. It was a mile or so out of town on Lorton Road but with easy access to the A66. It had a couple of fields where Mirk could walk and the room was in the courtyard, so there were no stairs to climb. The next day we parked the car in the town centre and, taking Mirk with us, turned into Main Street. I immediately felt that, yes, this was it! This was the place for me, and I told Louise that we need look no further. The majority of the shops on Main Street were independent, family-run businesses. There was a bookshop, shoe shops, newsagent, bakers, several hairdressers, restaurants and pubs, and of course, Wordsworth House and Garden with the National Trust Shop.

We pottered along the Main Street and into the Market Place where we stumbled into Neo's, an artist's dream of a coffee shop with a stone floor (and dog friendly). The coffee was great too. Some of the artwork was really interesting; sculptures made from spoons and other utensils; a wrought-iron chair with its legs sunk into wellington boots! All this art was made by a chap called Ben.

The following day we went to Buttermere and walked by Crummock Water before driving over to St Bees, a small coastal village. Mirk loved it, but he kept forgetting that he could not drink the seawater! The following day was spent back in Cockermouth, peering in estate agents' windows, visiting Neo's again and getting very excited about my dream becoming reality. I felt very much at home in this town. Perhaps it was the fact that the Christmas lights were on and the decorations made the town look very welcoming. We ate at Tarantella's, an Italian restaurant on the Main Street, before returning to the B&B.

***

Back home in Durham it was time to get my house shipshape before putting it on the market in the spring. As the economy was in a state of collapse, there was no telling how long this would take. But what I did know, was that Mirk was just as excited as I was! Over the coming year we visited Cockermouth every few months, including the week in November 2009 when the floods came.

We arrived on the Monday, staying in our usual B&B; then on Thursday 19 November, we moved into a friend's holiday cottage very near the town for a further three days. It had rained steadily all day on the Wednesday, and as Mirk and I attempted to walk along the riverside opposite Jennings Brewery, the river had already spread over the path preventing us from doing so. Retracing our steps, we dried out back at the cottage.

On that same Thursday, I had an appointment to view a bungalow in Maryport. Part of the road leading from Cockermouth to the A66 was already flooded, but cars were gingerly driving through, so I followed their example. The viewing over, I drove back and thought about the bungalow. It had a pitched roof but not with tiles or slates – just asphalt. I felt uneasy, unsure and needed to seek advice. It was 11.15am, and the road into Cockermouth was now cordoned off and the police were diverting traffic further along the A66 to the 'Sheep & Wool' roundabout to drive into the town. It continued to rain steadily.

We went back to the cottage for lunch, then ventured out again for a walk. This time we crossed the cobbles opposite the cottage, cutting through between the Georgian houses adjacent to each other and along the path to a small park between the Kirkgate Centre car park and Butt's Fold on St Helen's Street, one of the oldest streets in the town. We crossed a small footbridge over the Bitter Beck and turned right, walking for almost a mile to where this road meets Castlegate Drive, opposite Cockermouth School. Turning left here, and walking past a field of sheep, we paused briefly at a gate. From here, on a clear day there are some good views over the town to the right, and the Lorton Fells on the left, but today it was far too cloudy and wet, so we did not linger.

Heading on towards the town, with the rain still falling, we were both saturated, despite decent waterproofs and Mirk's tri-coloured fur coat. He kept stopping to have a good shake. On reaching the castle, we turned right down towards Jennings Brewery, but as we were nearing the entrance to the Brewery Visitors Centre, a woman was running across the area in front shouting something quite inaudible. We'd probably better not go there, I thought, so retraced our steps a little and turned right at the top by The Quince & Medlar. This is an extremely good vegetarian restaurant and is highly recommended. A drink on your arrival, a two- or three-course meal, and after-dinner drinks will pass a very pleasant 2-3 hours, and would be worth every penny.

From the restaurant we continued downhill and into the Market Place on the left, walking past Percy House, the oldest building in town. This lovely building houses a fabulous array of art, sculpture and jewellery, cards and woollen items, all neatly arranged in a small area with some interesting original features. It is thought to have been built in 1598 by Henry Percy, the 9th Earl of Northumberland. However, subsequent tests carried out by English Heritage researchers, using a study of tree rings, showed the house to be much older. The roof timbers revealed that the earliest Percy House timbers were dated around 1390. At the time the house was built, the first floor and ceiling would not have existed. This period of building is known as the 'open hall' style, the room being open to the roof to show off the craftsmanship in the roof timbers and arched braced collar roof trusses. In 1598, following a major revamp of the building, a unique ornate plaster ceiling and other features were installed, as was the fashion of the period. There are exposed oak beams, stone flags and Tudor and Victorian fireplaces, together with ancient nooks and ledges.

We continued along Main Street and over the bridge which spans the River Cocker as it bends around the next corner to meet the River Derwent. I glanced over the bridge to my right to see that the outdoor terrace along The Honest Lawyer restaurant was now underwater. It was 2.15pm.

"Oh dear," I thought, "so no sitting outside there for a coffee today!"

Hurrying past, all along the Main Street people were going about their everyday business, totally oblivious to the rising river levels. The Environment Agency had a lorry full of sandbags which were being distributed to shop owners, but at this point there seemed to be no urgency. We reached Wordsworth House and Garden, crossed the road, and doubled back along Main Street until we reached Lowther Went. We turned up here, passing the shops, crossed the road and turned right and round the corner into Sainsbury's car park. At the far end of the store, I tied Mirk up and went inside. After using the facilities, I selected a few items, placed them in my rucksack, and returned to Mirk.

By now, every item of clothing was completely drenched; my waterproofs were no longer waterproof! I decided I must buy some wellingtons, and as I crossed at the traffic lights, I looked down Station Street to find it cordoned off halfway down, just past the Co-op. By now people were huddled in small groups staring down the street, not able to believe that the whole of Main Street, the primary shopping street in the town, was submerged in several metres of water! I went into a shoe shop, but unsurprisingly they had virtually sold out of all their wellington boots. The helpful assistant directed me to the Farm and Agriculture shop just the other side of the traffic lights so I hastened up the steps with Mirk in tow. Once inside, he had a good shake over some large packets of dog food.

I spotted the wellingtons just near the door, and the kind assistant helped me select a pair, and we chatted while I changed into them. When I told her about the flooding in Main Street she was surprised, as less than an hour before business was much as usual. I kept my new wellies on, and new socks too, and while paying for them Mirk was praised and rewarded for his "good behaviour", and awarded accordingly by the assistant: "Some dogs would have almost destroyed the shop by now!"

The walk back to the cottage took us back to the traffic lights. We turned right into Lorton Street walked over Jubilee Bridge onto Victoria Road to the top, then turned left into Kirkgate and down to the cottage near the bottom, just before All Saints Church. Drying off took ages; I placed a towel over Mirk and rubbed, and rubbed and rubbed, and eventually he looked drier and respectable again. Meanwhile, I exchanged wet clothes, which went straight into the washing machine, for dry ones.

When I settled down later to watch the evening news, Cockermouth dominated both the national and local programmes, and I couldn't believe just how much damage had occurred both here and further west near the coast at Workington. Here, a bridge had collapsed into the river, and a policeman, Bill Barker, was swept to his death, while trying to protect the public from danger.

A while later, I thought I heard a dripping noise and an investigation found that, indeed, there was rain-water leaking through the ceiling and onto the landing carpet. I found a bucket, and placed it under the drip. Needing this to be resolved, I called the owner of the cottage, Alan, who gave me the number of a friend, Nelson, who lived opposite, and said that he would sort it out. I quickly called him and he arrived soon after, saying that he would have builders round in the morning, assuring me that he had a key to let them in, should I be out walking Mirk. Before he left he made a slit in the ceiling wallpaper to allow the excess water to fall into the bucket. All the time, Mirk, having been dried, fed and watered, just lay contentedly on the rug, blissfully unaware that today we had been part of events which would shape the social history of Cockermouth.

The following morning we were out at dawn, and along the cycle path past the cemetery. Overhead, the noise of a Sea King helicopter helping in the rescue operations brought my attention back to the events of yesterday. Today was Friday 20 November, and the town would normally be busy. But today in the Market Place, instead of shoppers were groups of mountain rescue teams and several television and radio reporters all eager to hear individual accounts of yesterday's unbelievable events.

The normally benign and familiar landscape of the streets had been transformed. The electricity was cut off in the nearby hotels and many of the neighbouring shops. The doorways of Lily & Co and the florist shop were blocked off entirely by debris dragged along by the rising waters and deposited there, preventing access. Looking left towards the bridge, there was a long table displaying a candelabra, deposited and left standing by the force of the rivers. Police and mountain rescue volunteers from far and wide were waiting for further instructions, as firemen joined in to rescue people from their homes down the vennel between

Banks the ironmongers and Beryl's, the hairdressers. The people who had been recently rescued stood quietly on the pavement, looking shocked and bewildered. *Now what?* – they must have been thinking – *What happens now?*

Over the weekend, people began to organise themselves, and some shops were able to relocate in Mitchells the Auctioneers who kindly allowed their units to be used. The two chemists, Allisons and Boots, worked to make sure that prescriptions were delivered to anyone in need. On Sunday morning, after the council had totally cleaned the roads of all debris, people were able to move about more freely, but all vehicle access was denied in Main Street in order that the contractors, builders, electricians and other tradesfolk could assess the damage. All of Main Street and the shops in Station Road were off limits. Even the businesses not directly affected by the floodwater were indirectly affected due to their loss of revenue.

At 9.30am on Sunday I attended a service in All Saints Church, directly behind the cottage. The mood was solemn. One family told of their home being flooded – just one of hundreds in the town. Later, the following statistics were recorded:

Over a 24-hour period, on the 19th/20th November 2009, 12 inches of rain fell; 200 people were rescued; 50 people were winched to safety; 691 homes were flooded; 226 businesses were flooded, which was 80%; water levels reached 10 feet; both the Gote and Cocker Bridges were closed; and 198 households were displaced long term. (Source: Cockermouth Flood Trail leaflet.)

The following morning, out earlier than I thought, I stopped to speak words of encouragement to the police officers standing on the corner behind Sainsbury's, opposite Junipers, a café and restaurant often frequented by Mirk and me. These officers were among 30 from Barrow who came in each evening to do the night shift. They were eagerly awaiting the end of their shift and were looking forward to their bacon butties! Just then, a vicar hurried round the corner and on seeing me, asked, "Do you want an egg sandwich?"

"No thanks," I replied.

"Do you have electricity?" she asked.

"Yes, thank you," I replied, so she smiled and scurried away. I thought to myself, *what energy she must have; she must have been up all night making those sandwiches and now she's going round distributing them. Whatever church she's from, then count me in!* Back in the cottage, I learned that the A66 was now open again near Keswick, so I packed up and left. It was incredibly sad to be leaving the town so soon after this disaster, and I had tears in my eyes as I approached the A66 at the 'Sheep & Wool' roundabout. The residents of Cockermouth had to get on with whatever they needed to do, rescuing their businesses and renovating their homes, and to return the town to its former self. I knew that Mirk and I would be back, and the floods, while they had destroyed homes and workplaces, had not deterred me from settling there.

***

In mid-February 2010, we returned to Cockermouth for a few days, and this time Louise came back too. We stayed at the same B&B, and Jeanette told us how the town was recovering. So it was that, fourteen weeks after the floods, Louise and I walked down Main Street at around 10.30am. The town was quiet, scarcely any people about. The road was still 'off limits' to vehicles apart from the working contractors and the many skips, now piled high with rubbish as ruined objects were removed from buildings. The builders, electricians and contractors had been hampered in the months afterwards, not only by delays with insurance assessors, but also by the severe weather conditions. There had been a lot of unexpected snow and freezing temperatures. Only businesses in large companies like the banks, Boots and Greggs were operational, while the many independent shops, run by the local people, had not been able to recover so quickly. Many of them had managed to relocate to the Tithe Barn at the top of Station Road, including Brysons the bakers, the New Book Shop, Allisons the Chemist and The Linden Tree. Apart from the Co-op and the Post Office, very few other shops were open.

Skips lined the Main Street on both sides and pipes stuck out of letter boxes in an attempt to rid the buildings of the moisture. A few more people were about now and viewed the artwork by the local school children which adorned the boarded-up shops. Pictures of the Sea King helicopters, lifeboats, dinghies and mountain rescue vehicles were displayed with words of support and prayers for the speedy recovery of the town. Even the Main Street post box was closed for business. The memories of that November day were still very vivid, and I had tears in my eyes at seeing how slowly the work of recovery was progressing. Louise and I went to Junipers for coffee, leaving Mirk safely tied to the lamp post outside where we could see him from the window.

Mirk and I returned again in late April, accompanied by my younger daughter Emily. We were going to Cockermouth to view several rented properties to see if we could find something suitable. By this time I had already sold my house and my moving day was set for June 1st 2010. This time, walking along Main Street with Emily, with the sun shining down on us, there was welcome evidence that the town was beginning to recover. A card shop had opened, its door ajar, inviting people in, and even though we had Mirk, this could not be ignored. It was spacious and light and the assistants were delightful. Further along, the National Trust shop had reopened, and on the opposite side of the road, the furniture store was open for business, although the carpet section was still closed. We had lunch at Junipers, sitting outside this time, and Mirk was made a fuss of, as he was, by now, a frequent and well-known visitor.

Driving to the coast, we visited Maryport, but Emily, being on various medications at that time, slept away the afternoon in the car. So it was just Mirk and I who took a leisurely stroll along the promenade. Whilst the beaches cannot compete with the Northumbrian coastline, the views across the Solway towards Dumfries and Galloway were stunning in the warm afternoon sun. Mirk was off his lead, trotting ahead on the path running parallel to the promenade. Suddenly, he spied another dog on the other side of the wall. It was a Dalmatian. Both dogs simultaneously stood on their hind legs, front paws on either side of the wall and sniffed each other's noses! Then, Mirk was off round the other side of the wall, sniffing around where two fishermen were casting out their lines. He dived nose-first into a tub of bait and picked up whatever was in there, getting caught on a hook in the process. While backing away, he dragged the line with him. Mirk was now trying to free himself, frantically pawing at his face, trying to get the hook out of his mouth and becoming more distressed and scared as he did so. One of the fishermen came over to help and with some teamwork, I managed to hook my finger under Mirk's blue collar and pull him to the ground. The man then carefully freed the hook from his mouth. Afterwards Mirk was very subdued but otherwise fine, and with him firmly back on his lead, we continued on our way.

We walked along to the golf course at the end of the promenade, and returned to the car. Mirk was still looking very sad, and I wondered if he had hurt himself. I decided to call in at the vets' to have him checked over, just in case. It would be as well to have him registered, in any event.

Back in Cockermouth, I explained Mirk's misadventure to his new vet and Mirk was given two injections; a painkiller and antibiotics in case of any infection, but thankfully the vet could see no evidence of any damage in Mirk's mouth.

The following day, Emily and I visited Wordsworth House and Garden. The cellar had been converted into an exhibition area which displayed photographs of the events of 19th November 2009. Some files were also available to look at which contained individual accounts of people's experiences of the flood. Upstairs, from some bedroom windows, the River Derwent could be seen flowing steadily past beyond the terrace at the far end of the garden. Here I watched as volunteers were busy at work, restoring the flowerbeds and sorting out the box hedges. I wondered to myself if perhaps I too, once I was fully settled in Cockermouth, could become a garden volunteer?

Preparation

During the next 17 months, I continued with my usual routine, which had been established following my retirement in February 2008, after 23 years as a probation officer. Six months prior to retiring, I had reduced my hours down to three days a week due to serious coccyx problems, which meant that sitting for long periods of time was extremely painful. I discovered and joined a local conservation group which met weekly, and although some of the work was quite strenuous, it was also very satisfying and enjoyable. Once Mirk came along, he too, became part of the group, and there were often other dogs there as well. Molly, an older golden retriever, just loved the sea and she and Mirk would have great fun splashing in and out of the water. Occasionally, Mirk would have a 'sleepover' with Molly, who, I believe, was not too happy about sharing her home and owners, Pat and Colin, with another dog!

The work along the Durham coast meant a lot of litter picking, repairing footpaths and steps, and generally cutting back on invasive species. In the summer, hay-making took place and lasted two to three weeks. The dogs would enjoy the freedom of the fields, and would not wander too far away. Mirk loved meeting not only other dogs but also people, whom he always needed to keep together, his herding instinct taking over. On one occasion when we were clearing a stream, running alongside a footpath, Mirk would run from one end of the group to the other. If someone went to the vehicle for tools, then Mirk would go too and made sure they came back into the group. Other people also liked having the dogs around, and would break off to play with them. One of our favourite places was Crimdon Dene which had a caravan park. It was here that Trevor had a hut and three black Labradors. He used it as an information centre during the migration season, when the little terns came over to breed, making their nests in small hollows in the sand. Each year, the conservation volunteers, together with people from other agencies, The National Trust, Natural England and Durham Heritage Coast, to name but a few, would gather to erect a fence on a certain section of the beach to help protect these birds from predators. However, some were very determined.

Hedgehogs wrecked the site one year by getting underneath the wire fence. Kestrels would hover overhead before diving to snatch their prey. The adult little terns would react as soon as a predator was spotted by calling loudly and flying around to divert the kestrels' attention. It was interesting to watch how, on one occasion, a ringed plover tricked a kestrel by pretending to have an injured wing. The little terns used this diversion to protect their nests whilst the ringed plover then flew off.

Keeping the coastline clean and free from litter was a mammoth task. It mainly came from four sources; rubbish dumped at sea, fishermen, tourists and rubbish from the local community, either accidental or deliberate. My very first experience of beach litter was in 2004, whilst on holiday in Portsmouth with a friend Joyce and her King Charles spaniel, Cecily. We were walking along the beach at Bognor Regis one afternoon when I noticed a typist's chair on the beach. This registered as being unusual, but we were so busy talking that I ignored it. A little later, as the tide was coming in, we turned and retraced our steps. On the way back I was amazed to see the chair was now being taken out to sea and I was so upset that I hadn't rescued it before. I took a photograph of it and it remained at the back of my mind until, several years later, I discovered the Marine Conservation Society and their 'Adopt a Beach' scheme. I joined in an annual beach litter-pick at Seaham. Duncan, a ranger of our conservation group, had heard that I was looking for a beach to clean, and he suggested that I could be responsible for a small bay by the harbour at Seaham. So with permission granted, I took on the task of spending every Monday morning collecting litter from the beach.

It was a protected area designated as a Special Site of Scientific Interest, on account of the colonies of breeding seabirds on the cliffs. It had a slope and steps leading down and, every time I visited, both sides of the steps would usually be covered in rubbish. Local young people and adults would frequent these areas and leave all their litter behind them. When the tide was out, rock pools were revealed and these were a fascinating place for adults and young children alike. For a year, Mirk and I collected beer cans, plastic bottles, fast-food containers, cartons, disposable nappies and plenty of broken glass bottles. I had seen teenagers using them as part of a game; once the bottle was empty it was placed on a rock a short distance away, and the youths would then take turns throwing stones at it until it was hit, thus smashing it to the ground. Needless to say, the glass went everywhere, and the countless tiny shards were impossible to pick up. Occasionally, I would come across syringes too, and special care would be taken to pick these up and dispose of them responsibly.

Mirk's first impression of the sea was that it was not good for drinking! He was not a swimmer, but would love to splash around, lie down in it, then run back onto the sand where he shook himself dry. Mirk also discovered that plastic bottles were jolly good fun to run around with, only to discard them as soon as he picked up a new and interesting scent. He was fascinated by the seaweed and tried to eat it, so much so that on one occasion he made himself sick. Fortunately, we were still on the beach collecting litter with some local cub scouts whom I had been invited to talk to about my beach-cleaning activities. Sometimes, Mirk would forget he was in the sea, and lick the water before remembering. Big mistake! He would shake his head, trying to rid himself of the taste.

As Mirk was a mature dog it was more difficult to teach him new tricks. I tried to get him to put each plastic bottle into a bin liner when he had finished with it, but alas, to no avail. One day he found a lovely medium-sized purple ball which he carried around in his mouth. He loved to chase after it if I threw or kicked it. Unfortunately, it didn't last very long, and in the end he destroyed it, though I prefer to think he simply loved it to death! Undeterred, he was off again to see what other discoveries he could make. He was never interested in sticks or stones, thank goodness, but loved his frisbee. He would race after it, often going beyond it as he would be running so fast that he overtook it! He loved to carry it back in his mouth, his head held high, but often it would never reach me as Mirk would just drop it the moment a new smell was detected and hurry off in its direction, leaving me to retrieve the frisbee.

After a year of beach cleaning, both alone and with a group of volunteers, I felt it was time that the locals not only became more aware of, but also took some responsibility for their own community. Litter was not only an eyesore to visitors, but also damaging to the wildlife and the environment. I spoke to the local councillors about a 'plastic-bag-free Seaham', and they were very welcoming of my proposal. The campaign was launched the following year with their support – not just financial, but also in the use of their committee room. Five friends and supporters offered to help and a committee was formed.

Two public events were held, one in the spring and one in the autumn, the launch to the public in May and the National Plastic-Bag-Free Day in September. These were held at the local shopping centre precinct. There were displays for the work of the Marine Conservation Society together with a video telling the story of how Modbury in Devon became the first town to be plastic bag free and why this was important. As Mirk was allowed inside the mall on these occasions, he was a valuable asset. People may have passed by the MCS posters, but Mirk they could not ignore. So, while listening to tales of their dogs past and present, and sharing a chat about Mirk and his adventures I was also able to tell them about the reasons behind the campaign and get them on board.

Freebies were readily available and my daughter Louise sold cotton bags which she had designed and painted with seascapes and other designs. I gave two local radio and newspaper interviews and received positive feedback from both. But sadly the idea never really caught on, despite the best efforts of John, the centre manager, and his helpful staff. Large supermarket chains had their own agendas, and while seeming to give us active support, they carried on distributing their plastic bags as usual.

By the end of 2009, it was time to hand over the beach to another volunteer, Michael, who was a local man, and therefore in a better position to pursue not only the problem, but also the solution. A bit disheartened, but by no means defeated, I moved on. But who knows, in the future some people may still remember 'Jean's Beach' as it was fondly referred to, and remember the fun we had, the people we met, and the artwork created by Louise and volunteers from beach litter that they had collected.

***

A yearly trip was arranged by Mark, one of the rangers, by way of a thank you to the volunteers. We went by mini bus to Seahouses, a small fishing village on the Northumberland coast. From the harbour, we caught a boat to the Farne Islands and landed to see the puffins, razorbills, guillemots, arctic terns, cormorants and kittiwakes. The first time I had visited was before getting Mirk. I felt really upset by our intrusion into the birds' 'maternity wards', and I vowed not to visit again. The chicks were so close to the path and whilst they were so easy to see and photograph, I felt uncomfortable around the arctic terns. It was not as bad by the clifftops as the razorbills, guillemots, kittiwakes and cormorants were out of reach of visitors. The puffins were in a separate area as they nest in burrows but were near enough to the visitors to be observed. Once Mirk arrived, we, along with a couple of other volunteers, walked along the beach from Seahouses to Bamburgh Castle, about three miles, and into the village for refreshments at 'The Copper Kettle', where Mirk was admired by the other tea drinkers. I don't think so many people would have spoken to me, had I not had Mirk. He was a real 'people dog' and everyone warmed to him and was fascinated by his story.

We were later collected by Mark and taken back to Seahouses where we all enjoyed fish and chips overlooking the harbour. The weather always seemed to be kind to us, and other trips included Beadle Bay and a walk to 'The Ship Inn' at Low Newton. It was on this occasion that a group member spotted a male otter swimming up the Long Nanny Burn, which we had just crossed by a small bridge. Mirk loved being on the beach where there were always interesting smells, especially in the seaweed. He was also a very good traveller, and never barked. Being a rather large Border collie, however, he did take up most of the space on the floor of the minibus!

Another of Mirk's favourite walks was around the various paths and nature reserves at Aykley Heads in Durham. Part of the path ran alongside the railway line and on the other side were two ponds. Mirk would head directly for these and whilst he made no attempt to swim, would lie flat in the water to cool off. We loved this walk as it was on several levels and every so often there would be a seat where I could sit and rest, admiring the view of Durham Cathedral in front of me. It was a great place to meditate, pray, and just to be.

Walking onto the higher level brought us to a circular walk leading to the Durham Light Infantry Museum. Mirk would always be several yards ahead and ready to meet and greet everyone and anyone. Being off the lead gave him the freedom to roll around in the undergrowth and poke his nose into bushes and even down rabbit holes, of which there were plenty. Attached to the DLI was a friendly café which we often frequented. Around the next corner was the entrance to the actual museum, which had automatic glass doors. On one occasion, Mirk was ahead of me and stood too close to the doors, and when I arrived he was already inside the museum, looking a bit bewildered! I stood close enough for the doors to open and, much to Mirk's relief, he was back outside once again.

Other favourite walks were around Durham City and exploring the paths between Shincliffe Village and the city along by the river. A circular walk could be started from the city, taking the steps down by Elvet Bridge and walking to Maiden Law Sports Centre Bridge, then crossing it to walk back to the city along the other side of the river. Then, of course, it would be time for some refreshments and to meet with friends. A favourite meeting spot was Vennels Café, and as the name suggests, it was situated up a vennel – a passageway between the gables of two buildings. With outside seating and adequate heaters, it was a pleasant place with good coffee and food, and a dog water bowl.

The other route would mean free parking in a lane by Houghall College and from there you could either go up the lane towards the college and the Houghall Trail, or cross over the A177 and take either path either side of the bridge. These would lead you into the city, via the previous walk where you could enjoy refreshments at the halfway stage of the walk. It isn't far, about 1½ miles, and walking into the city from Shincliffe gives you great views of Durham Cathedral and Castle. For a longer walk, ignore the steps to the town, and continue along the riverbank. Circular walks lead back into the city which can be accessed by the many bridges that span the River Wear.

Dumfries and Galloway

For Mirk's first anniversary, I decided to treat him to a few days away, back on his own territory. We drove to Crossmichael, staying at a B&B that I had used when I had first visited the area. It is on the Red Kite Trail, and so we visited Bellymack Farm from where the red kites are fed at 2pm every day of the year. It was also where I discovered that Mirk needed a new home! It is here that Todd, Mirk's brother, lives. He and Mirk are very much alike in looks and in temperament. The owners were delighted to see Mirk and to hear that he had settled so well.

The birds were magnificent! With a wingspan of almost 5½ feet (2 metres) and body weight of only 2-3lbs (approximately 1kg), they are agile and are able to stay in the air for several hours, hardly beating their wings. These birds are not particularly strong or aggressive; they are primarily scavengers and opportunists, although, of course, they are also predators, and can take a wide variety of live prey – from earthworms to small mammals, birds and amphibians. The red kites first breed when they are 2-3 years old and mate for life. Whether this is due to an attachment to the same geographical area and, therefore, nest sites, rather than a commitment to each other, is unknown. To watch the birds in flight and feeding from the table set out in the middle of the field is just awe-inspiring. They dive in by folding their wings, just skimming the table to snatch with their talons whatever is on offer before rising suddenly to find clear air space where the bird feels secure enough to eat. It does this by bending its head down to take the food from its forward-lifting feet. Seeing great numbers is amazing; how they just seem to float around the sky, socialising with each other over lunch. They do, however, have a short life span of around four or five years.

I remembered that on my very first visit to this B&B, I had discovered the Red Kite Trail. Having visited Bellymack Farm on that occasion, on the following morning as I was preparing to leave, I was amazed to see, as I glanced up at the sky from my bedroom window, a red kite flying in front of the window, circling and gliding for several minutes. *He has come to say goodbye,* I thought to myself. Sometime later, on a visit to the Farne Islands with the Durham Conservation Volunteers, I retold this incident to the ranger, Mark. Before I even finished my story, he interrupted me saying, "Yes, he came to say goodbye!" Amazing!

The following day, we made our way over to the RSPB reserve along the A710 at Mersehead. Here there is car parking along a track – and a visitor centre providing both refreshments and a good viewing area. There is a very pleasant circular walk, alongside a field which leads down onto the beach. A leisurely stroll along the beach gives time to play and Mirk loved going in and out of the water, remembering this time not to drink it! The views were stunning over to the Lake District and the Solway Firth, so we lingered here for a while and took a break.

There were several interesting features on the beach in terms of natural sculptures together with a man-made castle with shells placed down the centre. Continuing along, a signpost in the dunes points left along a path and back to the centre. Mirk and I then drove further along the coast to Rockcliffe. After a stroll around its small bay, we made our way to a tea shop with tables and seating outside where we decided to sit. Water is provided here for the dogs, and I passed the time of day chatting with other dog owners. Then a couple, having finished their refreshments, got up to leave the tea room, and passed our table on their way out. The lady saw Mirk and came across to make a fuss of him. I started to tell her how, the previous year, we had 'found' each other and she immediately said,

"Oh it's Mirk, isn't it?"

"Yes, how did you know?" Amazingly, it turned out that the couple have a holiday home in the area and visit frequently. They had heard about Mirk and she had wanted to take him, but as she already had two dogs, she had decided against it. She was now, however, delighted to know that Mirk and I were very happy together, and that she knew the end of that particular 'tail'.

The next day we drove over to Threave Castle, Gardens and Estate. Whilst dogs are not allowed in the gardens, there is an estate walk which is perfectly well signposted and lasts for around an hour. Dogs can then be fastened up outside the visitor centre shop and restaurant, where the coffee and food are always first class. We then went off to find the sculptures, about half a dozen or so by Rodin and Henry Moore which are privately owned and set on farmland. We only managed to see five before having to head back. It was good to see *Art in Nature, The King & Queen* and *John the Baptist* adding interest to the landscape.

Stopping on the way home the following day we called into Caerlaverock Castle and enjoyed a walk around the grounds and wood, before heading home.

Mirk

At 7 weeks old

The day after arriving in Durham

In Whinlatter Forest - Dec 2010

Gazing fondly at Durham Cathedral

On Crimdon Dene Beach, Co. Durham

Louise in Houghall Woods, Durham

Emily on a day out at Gibside, NT

The Family

Jean and Mirk, Durham – summer 2009

Mmm... sheep... - Dumfries and Galloway

'Work' and Play

Mirk and Molly - Crimdon Dene Beach

Art & Environment

Mirk at a litter pick on Seaham Beach after finding a purple ball

In the Lake District

Fleetwith Pike, Buttermere

Cockermouth Floods

The morning after... Friday 20 November 2009

Happy Times...

Mirk and Poppy - July 2013

Mirk - resting during play

Mirk Goes to Mull

Whenever luggage appears in the porch, Mirk knows that he is in for another trip. He lies between the front door and the porch, so that he is ready and waiting in his tri-coloured coat and collar. There is no chance of him being left behind, as I can't get out of the door without almost tripping over him! Because he is being an obstruction, I put him in the car first along with his bedding, bowls and food. For this particular trip of around ten days or so I had invested in a harness which had two small bags on either side in which to put Mirk's water bowl, treats, poo bags, a small towel and a ball. This was my attempt to help Mirk take responsibility for his belongings. Big mistake! A trial walk by the banks of the River Wear proved to be a disaster. The harness would not stay centrally on his back and the movement when he walked, or rather trotted, meant that it moved from side to side. No matter how much I tried to tighten this around his middle it was never secure enough. Adjusting the contents of the bag also proved difficult. The problem might be solved if only he would drink his water, I thought. Nonetheless, I packed it all the same!

This trip was along the north-east coast, staying at Coldingham and then on to St Abbs, before taking the Edinburgh bypass to just north of Stirling where we would stay overnight with my best friend, Yvonne, who was to join us for the holiday on the Isle of Mull. Mirk loves new places, and revisiting old ones. He is always eager to explore lanes and tracks and to greet new people. He is an excellent traveller, always eager to get into the car; and once the car is in motion he settles down to sleep. Everything is an adventure to Mirk.

Arriving at Yvonne's, Mirk waited in the car until he was told he could leave. He made a huge fuss of Yvonne, and she of him. Having had dogs for most of her life, although at this point she didn't have any, Yvonne easily warmed to Mirk. Not to be completely bereft of animals, she did own a cat called Pusscat. Mirk quickly spied her, but made no attempt to chase her, as she jumped up onto the stone wall which separates the river from the lane running up past the four cottages. Pusscat accompanied us as we started up the lane, but she walked along the wall for as far as it goes, before jumping down and running along the lane in front of us. She was very wary of Mirk and kept her distance, but Mirk was far more interested in smells than Pusscat. Pusscat did not like Mirk very much, but she nonetheless liked me. I knew this for sure, when the very next morning I found a dead mouse underneath my chair. How kind of Pusscat to provide my food, although in the end, I opted for the toast and cereal!

I love being at the cottage with the River Teith running alongside it, and the sound of the constant flow of water, splashing as it tumbles its way downstream. I find it soothing and restful and always sleep with the window open.

The next day, we travelled north west to Oban where we caught the ferry to Mull. I had been a couple of times before, but they had not been very successful trips. This time, I was hoping that I might see a white-tailed eagle and also have a boat trip to do some wildlife watching. As Yvonne did not enjoy being on small boats, or planes for that matter, she was more than happy to look after Mirk for a few hours.

The sea crossing on the ferry was tranquil enough, and Mirk took this all in his stride. On deck, he paid attention to each row of seats, seeking out new and more interesting smells round every corner. He was always very well behaved, and when we returned to the dog area below, he just settled down to rest. Getting Mirk to and from the car was more stressful for him. The cars were packed quite close together, not allowing much room to manoeuvre, and he needed some space in order to jump into the car. The fumes and noise were much more acute and Mirk hastily settled into the car, not wanting to linger.

I just love the idea of being on an island and here is what the late John Smith MP once said:

"There is a very special feeling about arriving on an island and seeing the boat depart. You are irrevocably part of the island, part of its community, bound into its very nature by its isolation."

I find this so true, not least of all when I took Yvonne to Islay a few years earlier. We had arrived by plane from Glasgow and drove into Bowmore by hire car only to see Lord Robertson walking across the square! As we enjoyed some lunch in a nearby hotel, Yvonne met a friend who told her that later on that day, the late John Smith's daughter would marry Lord Robertson's son. The church, as it turned out, was about a mile or so from our B&B. We duly turned up, parking along the grass verge, and leaving the keys in the ignition in case someone needed to move it later. We watched as the bride and other members of the wedding party arrived. We stayed to see them leave after the ceremony and lingered as the happy couple posed for photographs overlooking Loch Indaal, before leaving. It was so relaxed, and many other locals and visitors to the island chatted together with reporters and photographers. This experience, for me, really did capture what John Smith had said.

The drive to the holiday cottage was uneventful, stopping only once for refreshments at the gallery and café, and to give Mirk a walk.

On reaching the Treshniss Cottage, which was located on the north-west side of the island, Mirk enjoyed the freedom of his new surroundings. He rolled around on the grass in front of the cottage which overlooked the small isles of Coll and Tiree. There were sheep in the field beyond and Mirk stood and watched them for a while before settling down on the grass to sleep. The cottage was spacious; I placed Mirk's bedding in the lounge by the open door in order that he would have easy access to his water bowl, and he seemed very happy.

The week proved to be quite eventful. Yvonne's partner Rob arrived for a couple of nights, accompanied by his West Highland terrier, named Snowy. He was quite boisterous – Snowy, not Rob – and being only 2 or 3 years old, was still very playful and constantly required attention. Yvonne would take Mirk for his early morning walk with Rob and Snowy, which meant there was no rush to get up. I've never been one for staying in bed once I am awake, and it is always a pleasure to take Mirk out, especially in the early morning. However, I do like to share Mirk with my friends.

On Tuesday, we all drove down to Fionnphort to catch the ferry over to Iona. It was a long drive, as I had totally underestimated the time that it would take. Forty miles took us nearly two hours! We enjoyed a great day on Iona having walked to the north end of the island, with glorious weather, calm turquoise sea and sandy beaches. The dogs were in and out of the water and as we had taken lunch, we delighted in the tropical-like scenery. By the time we returned to the car at around 6pm, we needed to make haste as we had a table booked for 8pm at the Calgary Hotel. Driving off, I noticed a clonking noise which had not been there before, but as the car appeared to be running smoothly, I continued until I heard the offending part fall off. I stopped the car, and walked back to find half a coil spring lying in the road. Cautiously, we arrived back at the hotel with literally two minutes to spare. However, the dogs had not been fed, so I asked the waitress if there was any dog food available and explained our predicament. As the proprietors were dog owners, they were happy to oblige and brought out a large bag of dog food and some water. Table for five then!

After being fed the dogs lay down to sleep while the three of us enjoyed our meal and reflected on the day, and plans for the morning as we needed to take Rob to Craignure to catch his ferry back to Oban. The next day, driving slowly into Tobermory, I found a garage where the mechanic identified the problem. I then had to call the RAC and wait for a breakdown truck. Only forty minutes later the truck and driver had arrived – from Fionnphort! There were no available hire cars on the island, and as the part needed to come from Glasgow, it would be at least a couple of days. The lady at the Tourist Information Office was extremely helpful, allowing me the use of a telephone and also arranging another ferry, as we were booked on the 2pm on Saturday. The latest one was 7pm, which gave us an extra half day on the island. The RAC then arranged for a taxi to collect us from our cottage and take us to the garage to pick up the car. Meanwhile, Rob managed to get a bus to Craignure, so Yvonne, Mirk and I took the bus as far as Calgary as it went no further. Before we embarked on the three-mile walk back to the cottage, we enjoyed excellent tea and scones at the outside café-gallery at the hotel. The walk back by the beach was pleasant enough.

It was during this holiday that Mirk first encountered ticks. These tiny creatures latched themselves onto Mirk around his head and shoulders. It was only as a result of grooming Mirk each night that they were detected. Fortunately, the chemist in Tobermory had a good supply of small plastic implements, just made for this eventuality – a two-pronged fork at right angles to the handle, thereby removing these nasty creatures.

I never did get to see the white-tailed eagles, or otters or any other wildlife for that matter, but the island, as always, had stunning sunsets over Coll and Tiree and the big wide sky and sandy bays were enough to make us feel content.

Our final day, and sure enough a taxi arrived to take us and all our luggage to the garage to collect my car. A good drive, and this time I was able to look out for wildlife. Several hours later, we arrived at the harbour for the 7pm ferry.

After staying a night at Yvonne's, following last night's drive from Oban, I arranged to stay the following evening at her cottage on the River Tweed at Walkerburn, which we had visited before. A particular place that I had wanted to visit was on the way: Traquair House, Innerleithen, Scotland's oldest inhabited house. It dates back to 1107 when it was originally a hunting lodge for the Kings and Queens of Scotland. It later became a refuge for Catholic priests during the time when the Stuarts of Traquair supported Mary, Queen of Scots, and the Jacobite cause without counting the cost. Whilst I was only interested in the grounds for walking Mirk, together with the various craft workshops and 1745 Cottage Restaurant, nonetheless it was well worth the visit. After a couple of hours, having eaten lunch and walked along the many footpaths, we continued on our way, arriving at the cottage by late afternoon.

The following morning, rising early, Mirk and I walked along the path beside the River Tweed behind the cottage. I kept him on his lead because whilst I couldn't see any sheep, there were cattle on the opposite bank, some in the shallow edge of the river. We continued right along to a bridge, before returning the same way. (It is usual for Mirk to be kept on his lead if I am taking him to an unfamiliar place.) However, on the way back, we met an elderly man with a couple of border collies running free. He had a crook in his hand. He greeted us, asking:

"Why is your dog on a lead?" I explained why.

"No sheep here," he replied. Reluctantly, I unhooked Mirk's lead from his blue collar. Big mistake! In a flash, Mirk had vanished out of sight. We called him, and called and called. Just then, a steady stream of shorn sheep walked through a gap in the hedge and along the path and stood in line by a closed gate. They appeared unfazed; not bleating or looking distressed.

Then, just as quickly as he had disappeared, Mirk reappeared, dripping wet from a dip in the Tweed. He came and sat at my feet, looking up at me, as if to say, "Well, aren't I a clever dog?" Being so relieved, I hooked his lead onto his blue collar, said goodbye to the retired shepherd and went on our way. The sheep meekly went back from whence they came. I didn't know what to think. It was no good scolding Mirk, he had only done what he was born to do, and very well too, by the looks of it. With no harm done, I was relieved to be back at the cottage. I hastily packed and we left for home.

Tuesday 1 June 2010 – Move to Cockermouth

One fine day at the end of March, I received a call from the estate agents to say an offer had been made on my house. After further negotiations, it was finally sold, and a move was planned for between May and June. The day we moved out, Mirk went to spend time with some 'dog-friendly' friends, Biddy and Mike, leaving me free to manage the packing and removal operation. I did not want Mirk to witness this departure. For a few nights, Mirk and I stayed with a friend, Heather, and on Tuesday 1 June 2010, we said goodbye to Durham.

As I drove along the A66 towards Penrith, the fells were coming into view around every bend. Mirk, surrounded in the back with his belongings, remained alert, and I'm sure that on this occasion he must have thought: *This is more than just a few days away.* This time, we were to make our home in Cockermouth: make new friends and become part of the community.

We aimed to stay at the B&B, for a couple of days, to look for some rented property. There had been a telephone conversation and Jeanette had said that if I still had nowhere to live, they would sort out a caravan as a temporary measure. However, this took longer than expected, so after a couple of nights at Graysonside, we went to Ambleside for three nights until the caravan was ready. Mirk loved being back at the B&B and at least here, the place was familiar.

So a caravan it was then! It was small, old, but functional (and it brought back happy memories). Jeanette also thoughtfully provided a microwave, kettle and toaster. She thought that the "van was sub-standard" but Andrew thought it was fine, after all a contractor had last slept in it! I guess you can't argue with that! There was a small toilet block which housed two separate toilets and a shower room each. One had a sink for washing up in, and both were less than a minute away. The caravan was positioned by a fence, but the view of the Lorton Fells was wonderful. I slept on my side on one of the settees in my sleeping bag as all my bedding was in storage in Durham until I had found something more permanent. But Mirk loved the caravan; he would spend most of his waking hours outside by the open door just resting his chin between his paws or watching the rabbits as they grazed away the hours. Next to me were Yvonne and Steve, victims of the flood, who had spent the entire winter in their caravan and were almost ready to move back into their home.

The situation in Cockermouth with regards to housing was still uncertain as many residents were still in rented holiday homes or temporary accommodation with family or friends. As the weather was fine and Mirk was really at home, I decided that I would buy my own caravan and then look to rent a house over the winter months. So when my friend Fiona flew over from Hamburg to spend some time with her family in Scotland, we met up in Carlisle and I drove her to Dumfries and Galloway to stay with her and her dad for a few days. Her sister, Katie, also joined us at Carlisle and we drove back in convoy having stopped for refreshments at the hotel at Gretna Green.

Katie lived in Gatehouse of Fleet and I had met her before when Fiona and I had met on a National Trust working holiday two years earlier. On the way, we called into a large caravan retailer and looked at many caravans. Thinking that this was to be a short-term measure, I did limit myself financially, but there was nothing that really appealed. We went for lunch in the nearby town, over which we chatted and shared views on the pros and cons of the caravans we had seen. We were all new to this, but it was good to share my views with friends that I could trust. We returned later, and continued looking. I spotted one that was double what I expected to pay, but I knew that this one was for us. Decision made, the delivery was fixed for the first week in July as I was to go off to Iona at the end of June, with the National Trust for Scotland Thistle Camp.

The caravan duly arrived a couple of hours late and was set up. It was spacious, and had all we needed – somewhere to eat and sleep and enjoy just being. The site was small; most people just used it to store their caravans and motor homes and would come and collect them to holiday elsewhere. Some stayed though, and they became our new neighbours. Mirk would immediately go to greet them as soon as they alighted from their cars and would love it if a new dog jumped out too. Mirk had the freedom to be safe in an outdoor environment. There were picnic tables strategically placed by each plot overlooking the Lorton Fells: Grisedale Pike, Hopegill Head, Whiteside and Grasmoor. The delight of these fells was immeasurable; the light constantly changing as the clouds moved across the sky. I will never tire of this view, and family and friends who visit are also suitably impressed.

The day after I moved, I went to a local store to buy some bedding for the caravan and other household items like mugs and cutlery. Whilst there, a message was tannoyed throughout the store stating that the Cumbrian Police had issued a warning for everyone to remain indoors as there was a gunman further to the west randomly shooting at people, passers-by, even people in cars. His exact location was not known, as he was on the move. The store was to close, but people could remain or leave. I said that I had a dog in the car, and as it was unknown as to how long this would last, they kindly let me bring Mirk into the entrance, the large open part containing shrubs, pots and general gardening equipment, then produced a bowl of water. I then received a text from my daughter, Emily, asking me if I was all right and "not to walk Mirk" but to remain indoors. After I had been in Cockermouth during the floods, I guess some friends and family were concerned for my wellbeing. After almost an hour we left with our purchases and headed for the town and home. It was almost 1.30pm when it was announced that the gunman was no longer at large, eventually cornered in the Boot/Eskdale area.

Over the summer months, Mirk and I explored the local walks, mainly around the town, the cemetery, cycle paths and Harris Park. Here, we met many dog walkers, and Mirk was always well behaved. Once he had sniffed the dogs, he would usually wander off to find other scents. Sometimes he would want to play with them, other times he was content with his ball on a rope or frisbee, whichever I had brought along. Parking around the park was limited to an hour, but as Mirk trotted on ahead, we managed this comfortably. For the longer walks we would park on the Strawberry How Road where there were no restrictions and then enjoyed picking up the Coast2Coast cycle route, turning right or left through the cemetery to complete a loop. This would take longer if we stopped to rest in the cemetery and sit on a bench to watch the red squirrels. They were delightful to spot, scurrying from tree to tree or gravestone, ever alert and watchful. Here, there was an abundance of hazelnuts, so it was not surprising to see so many red squirrels there too!

By September, the caravan was becoming less inviting in the evenings as the light began to diminish earlier and earlier. Also, fewer folk visited, and only at weekends. The site felt more isolated, being some distance away from the B&B. It was time to look for a cottage for the winter months. I had earlier seen a sign on a cottage at the top of Kirkgate. One Monday morning, as the rain fell steadily, preventing me from doing my usual volunteering in the garden at Wordsworth House, I duly visited the agents. It was 10.40am. A viewing had been arranged for 12 noon, but I could go earlier. We immediately went along, and decided that this would be fine. Not only was it convenient for the town, but several friends also lived on this road. I went straight back to the office to complete the necessary forms and agree the tenancy.

We moved the following month, and Louise arrived to help. My belongings, which had been in storage in Durham, were at last being transported along the A66 to their final destination: Cockermouth.

Heading towards the town, we often turned left after Jubilee Bridge – signposted YHA – and down the steps to take the riverside path into Harris Park. A few metres further along there were steps leading up on to the redundant railway line which once carried goods and passengers from Workington to Keswick and further eastwards. From the bridge there were various options. We could turn left, across the bridge, then right to follow the wooded path which went into the open area of Harris Park. Either side of the River Cocker are branching paths which we soon knew well. It was here on the day after Bonfire Night that Mirk was either spooked or disorientated so much that we became separated. I had let him off the lead as we walked along the middle path, and usually when Mirk is ahead of me, he waits when he comes to a junction to see which way I tell him to go. But on this occasion – it was around 8.15am – he totally disappeared! I called and called, but there was no sign of him. Sometimes, he might see another dog in the distance or on a parallel path and go off, but then having said 'Hello', would linger until I arrived. I was then aware of a message on my mobile, saying that Mirk had been found trying to cross Lorton Road. (My mobile number is on Mirk's name disc.) The lady said she had managed to manoeuvre him away and that she had tied him up at the Methodist Church by the steps and that he was secure and safe. She explained that as she was due to attend a meeting at 8.30am she had had to leave him. I called her to thank her, and in tears, jogged my way back along the river path, turning right through a wrought-iron kissing-gate, down the path past Rubbybanks Cottage until I reached the steps leading up to Lorton Road. As I turned left, I caught sight of Mirk sitting on the top step by the church door, looking bemused. We were so pleased to see each other, and I was so relieved that he had been saved from the traffic. I guess that he must have been spooked or maybe heard a gunshot or something similar. As we had moved from the caravan into a cottage at the top of Kirkgate for the winter just a few weeks earlier, he would have been on his way home, as the top of Lorton Road meets Kirkgate just by the cottage before heading out of town. It was almost a week before Mirk was allowed off the lead again!

It was while we were at the cottage that we became very good friends with my neighbour, Kris. She still worked part-time, and had a Jack Russell called Fudge who barked incessantly at Mirk on each meeting. Her husband, Trevor, who was disabled, would be seen sitting in his chair by the window as we walked past. Kris and I would walk the dogs together on her non-working days of Monday, Wednesday and Saturdays. These walks became very therapeutic for both of us as we shared various aspects of our lives, complained about this and that and generally put the world to rights.

After about a week at the cottage, Emily came to stay after her sister, Louise had just left. I had a really sore throat, and my GP had given me antibiotics. A couple of days later, I returned, as my throat had worsened. She called a couple of hospitals in order to arrange an immediate assessment, and printed out a referral to produce at the hospital in Carlisle. As I expected to be home later in the day, I only took some cash and my mobile, and left Emily and Mirk together. Unfortunately, I was required to stay in, and so Trevor, who had very kindly taken me to the hospital, returned to Cockermouth. He called in to tell Emily and offered to walk Mirk the following morning.

That afternoon, Emily took Mirk for his walk in Harris Park. He was off his lead, and Emily followed Mirk along the path, believing that he would be showing her his usual route. Not so! Mirk, being the intelligent dog that he is, decided to give Emily a display of his herding skills – one that she will never forget. Cunningly, once across the bridge prior to the YHA Hostel, Mirk turned right instead of left and stood by the kissing gate. Emily opened the gate and continued along the path. To the left of the field there are sometimes cattle on higher ground. Unbeknown to Emily, the cattle had been replaced with sheep. Mirk took off and proceeded to herd them into a corner. Two sheep ran in opposite directions. Mirk left the flock, and brought the remaining two to join the rest of the sheep before returning to Emily. He sat at her feet, looked up into her eyes, as if to say: *See. That's what I'm good at! Aren't I a clever dog?* Poor Emily was distraught and frantic. No amount of calling him had made any difference. In fact, it had made matters worse as Emily, usually very confident around dogs, felt totally out of control. Needless to say, Mirk was put back on his lead and marched back home forthwith. That is, of course, when dear Emily eventually found her way out of the park, an hour and a half later! Bless.

***

A favourite walk from Kirkgate is along Cocker Lane, past the wee cottage by the bridge, over the bridge and left, to walk alongside the River Cocker. The walk continues under the bridge which takes the traffic along Lorton Road, and under a much longer bridge which once carried the railway line from the west coast to Keswick. We follow the river along the path to the end, turning right by Rubbybanks Cottage and into Harris Park. Keeping the river on our left Mirk usually hops down the bank, into the river, regardless of the temperature! He re-emerges, has a good shake, and trots off ahead of me. He never attempts to swim, but goes in and lies down, lapping up the water. Only on one occasion did I see him swim, and it was along the same stretch of river when he went in after another dog. However, the spaniel was chasing a stick, so swam out into the middle of the river. As I crossed over another bridge, I called to Mirk. He thought that I was still on the other side where he went in, so I guess I confused him. Unfortunately, he was unable to get out at my side, as the bank was too steep. He was then forced to swim back. At least I now know that he can swim!

Along the river are still remnants of the flooding, such as a tree trunk half on the bank, still covered in deposited rubbish, or trees with their lower branches littered with left-over river debris. Fortunately, the rivers appear to have made a good recovery. On one particular day I noticed three men leaning over the wall by the bridge, so I too leaned over to see some very large salmon in the relatively shallow, clean water. Herons often fly along the river, and a favourite spot for them is at the base of a small waterfall on the opposite side of the river, on a large boulder.

Mornings are a good time to spot dippers, with their white chests and tell-tale dipping movement of their heads. They are usually seen in pairs. On Christmas Eve, while walking with Louise, a kingfisher flew from one branch to another, almost level with us, before disappearing. The following day, after Louise had returned home, I called her when I reached the exact spot where the kingfisher was seen. I was just about to say that there was no kingfisher today when the family behind me, called, "There's a kingfisher." I glanced behind, just as he disappeared under the bridge. Further along, two men with long lens cameras had also seen the bird. Then suddenly, he flew along the river near the opposite side, landing on a branch of the tree. He watched the river for several minutes, before diving into the river to bring out a fish, which he ate on a nearby branch. It must have been his Christmas lunch! This was one of the best presents to see on Christmas Day and will remain with me for many years to come. No wonder there is a house further along the road called 'The Kingfisher'. Once you have seen a kingfisher in the wild, you will not forget it. How the brightest blue on earth was given to this bird must have been God's creation, and for me this is captured in the poem by William H. Davis;

The Kingfisher

'It was the Rainbow gave thee birth,
And left thee all her lovely hues,
And, as her mother's name was Tears
So runs it in my blood to choose
For haunts the lonely pools, and keep
In company with trees that weep.
Go you and, with such glorious hues,
Live with proud peacocks in green parks;
On lawns as smooth as shining glass,
Let every feather show its marks;
Get thee on boughs and clap thy wings
Before the windows of proud kings.
Nay, lovely bird, thou art not vain;
Thou hast no proud, ambitious mind;
I also love a quiet place
That's green, away from all mankind;
A lonely pool, and let a tree
Sigh with her bosom over me.'

I rediscovered Whinlatter, a place which I last visited in 2001 when I had taken my daughter, Emily, and her boyfriend, Michael, over to camp for a week at Keswick, at the Camping and Caravanning Club site. It was the first week that the footpaths had re-opened following the outbreak of foot-and-mouth disease, which also was the year that the osprey returned to Bassenthwaite Lake to breed. The visitor centre – with a CCTV camera to display live images of the birds on their nest -- was then located in the car park, with a small tea room nearby. Now, there is a new Siskin Café and shop and visitor centre housed in one large building. An area with information about the ospreys is located between the shop and the café, where excellent food is prepared. The seating area outside on the verandah is an excellent viewing platform from which to watch robins, chaffinches, all manner of tits and, of course, siskins.

In 2010, the osprey relocated their nest, so it was too late for the RSPB team to place cameras in time to project live images. Nevertheless, a walk through Dodd Wood to the two viewing platforms gives Mirk a good walk as we ascend uphill – first to the lower viewing point, then to the second which gives excellent views over Bassenthwaite Lake – the only real lake in the Lake District, as all the others are either meres or waters.

The nest can be seen quite clearly from the telescopes, and every so often an osprey would be spotted flying over the lake scanning for fish to be taken back to the nest to feed the two chicks. Further along the track is the summit of Dodd Fell, which is well worth the effort of the climb, which we did on one occasion, along with Helen. It is often busy, particularly on a nice day, but the views from the summit are spectacular, looking over towards Keswick and Derwentwater, to the side, Ullock Pike, Carlside, Skiddaw, and over towards Whinlatter and the Derwent fells of Barf, Lord's Seat and Sale Fell, and further round to Causey Pike. On the way up, however, Mirk began to limp, so we stopped and examined his paws, to find that a small clear plastic bottle top was stuck on one of his front paws. I removed it, and thankfully Mirk was fine. It continues to annoy me when people are so careless and thoughtless about the way they dispose of litter. I thought back to all the litter that I had previously collected on the beaches, and felt saddened at how irresponsible some people are in showing a total disregard not only for the welfare of dogs and other wildlife that give us so much pleasure but also for our environment. Mirk continued on his way, sniffing out all manner of new and interesting smells. Needless to say, he reached the summit cairn first, ahead of both Helen and me.

***

The Keswick Convention is held there over three weeks in summer. A friend from Durham, Dawn, together with her year-old West Highland terrier, shared a cottage with Mirk and me for a week. This is what Poppy thought of Mirk during our week together:

'After what seemed a long car journey, my owner let me out of my confined space and took me to a park where I could drink from the river and run around on my long lead. We then walked some streets and after my owner had spoken on her phone, we headed purposefully in one direction. My owner knew the other lady we met and I thought I had met the large dog in front of me. Anyway, being friendly, I approached him, but he just turned his head away. Huh! I hoped that, if I was going to spend more time with him, he would become more receptive and at least speak to me. Later that day, we went into a strange house, strange to me anyway. I had a good look around but the other dog, who I later discovered was called Mirk, just lay down in the lounge. Ah well. Nothing ventured, nothing gained. I approached him again. At least as he lay down he was more at my level. I ran my nose over his face, and talked gently with my tiny yelps asking him to play with me, and you would not believe what I received in return... he lifted his paw and dismissed me with it!

That evening, after another walk, we were left on our own for a while. Without my owner to protect me, I decided to keep my distance and rest at the other end of the kitchen where my bed had been placed. Around what would normally have been my bedtime, all these people came into the house. No one was much interested in me, and neither was Mirk, but he did pinch my favourite toy. I watched in dismay as Mirk chewed on MY apple. And he made it squeak. How did he do that? Then he chewed on my teething bone. I felt a bit sorry for him then as it made his gum bleed. I tried to show him I cared by approaching him, but he went to his owner for a fuss instead.

When we went for a walk in the park or up the hills, I was occasionally allowed off my lead. I began to see Mirk as a wiser dog than me, sometimes. I followed him and this led to several soakings in the river, as well as some lovely smells. However, sometimes he ran further than I thought I should go, to talk to some other big dogs. On these occasions, I sat back and watched from a safe distance. I did approach the smaller dogs though, which Mirk was not as interested in. I think one nipped his nose!

I remember one time when we walked by a lake, Mirk waded in. I duly followed but, although the water only came to the top of Mirk's legs, it nearly covered me. Then Mirk lay in the water – not me though! I was already cooled enough. Another time, I had run around with Mirk and bathed my face in some nice smelly stuff. My owner seemed disgusted with me and I could not understand what I had done that she did not like. I enjoyed the smell, but she put me in a sink and shoved my head under a tap! When we arrived home, I was shampooed and had water thrown at me to rinse it off. Why was it that I was always treated like this and Mirk was not? The worst he endured was having his legs wiped with baby wipes!

I did not give up on Mirk during the week. I was determined he would play with me. I rolled on my back for him, leapt at him, shared my toys with him and even slept next to him. The only time he ever acknowledged my presence was on a walk when he suddenly decided to chase me. My little legs were no competition for Mirk's long ones and I had to run to my owner for protection.

You know, I liked Mirk, in a strange kind of way. Although he was aloof with me, he was obviously sensitive and loving towards people, and particularly his owner. He taught me not to charge about all the time. For example, in the tea rooms we went into each day, I learned to sit quietly under the table, as Mirk did. I felt safe with him most of the time and he was rather like the father figure I never knew. I actually missed him when I got home and hope we will spend time together in the future. He might even get used to me one day! Who knows?'

***

Over the next eighteen months or so, Mirk and I explored not only the local walks and paths around the town but also how we could become part of the community, which would give us a sense of belonging. Remembering the move to Durham which I made with the girls in the summer of 1981, it was the church that provided friendship, fellowship, hospitality and support. Now, in Cockermouth, after visiting several places of worship, it was Christ Church that I chose. Gradually, I made new friends and became a member of a home group which was hosted and led by Trevor and Elizabeth.

Meeting with newly made friends in the town for coffee was a good way of getting to know people better and supporting the recently opened coffee shops which were popping up in the town. In return, I began to discover where I could be of use. Volunteering at Wordsworth House and Garden was a start, and with Amanda as our head gardener and her small group of about a dozen helpers, many happy hours were spent there during the summer months. As well as tending to the garden, we welcomed visitors and listened to their stories. Hens arrived and were given names by the local school children, adding much interest for the visitors.

The caravan overlooking the Lorton Fells was also an ideal place to meet and make new friends. Enid and Harold bought a caravan on site and so became frequent visitors and firm friends. People came from far and wide – some stayed only a night before moving on; others stayed much longer. Cyclists came to do the C2C route; some folk camped; motorcyclists from Scotland came to tour the area, wanting to know about the passes. Three young schoolboys from Winchester were cycling from Land's End to John O'Groats to raise money for a local children's hospice; two friends came to camp for Woolfest – an annual event celebrating anything to do with wool and sheep, of which there were plenty!

During the second half of 2011, as part of the church's fund raising committee, Mary, Phil, Dot and I organised a Strawberry Cream Tea and Wine event and Jeanette gave us permission to hold this in the field next to the caravan which overlooked the Lorton Fells. After a risky decision on the morning of the event to go ahead, despite the wet weather of late, I was confident that all would be well. And indeed by 4pm the sun was out making the event very inviting. To include Mirk in this I set a competition to guess Mirk's birthday. He sat obediently by the stall while folk had five chances for a £1 to guess the date. Elizabeth won the prize – a cuddly Border collie toy – which had been donated to Dot by Laura, who along with her Border collie, Jake were members of the Cockermouth Mountain Rescue Team. (These toy dogs are sold to raise money for the Search and Rescue Teams throughout the area of Cumbria.) Of the £400 raised in total, Mirk's birthdate competition raised £15. I sold some fingerless mitts and bags that I had made from wool from the sheep on the Cumbrian fells, and raised £60.

Jeanette from the B&B came along, also Enid who quickly made friends, and the children and adults played a game of rounders. After several hours, the event came to a close and it seemed to be a great success. People commented that they had been delighted not only with great food and drink set in a beautiful landscape, but also a very different kind of fund-raising event.

Alnmouth

The idea to live in Northumberland for three months over the autumn/winter of 2011/2012 came about when a friend mentioned that her daughter, Lucy and husband, Henry, were planning on spending some time in Thailand and Nepal. The couple were looking for someone to rent their second home in Shilbottle, near Alnmouth and I said that I might be interested. However, it wasn't until three months later that I ventured over to see them after receiving an email.

Our arrival in the middle of October found Mirk and me on the beach at Alnmouth – a place that I knew well from several weekend visits to The Friary there. We were enjoying the late afternoon sun, and it felt good to be back. Turning into the driveway of the house, the car suddenly became stuck as my wing mirror made contact with the wrought-iron gate. Stuck, then! I rang the next-door neighbour, although I knew she would be taking a yoga lesson, so it was a fruitless exercise. Not being able to open the car door either meant that I was well and truly jammed! Twenty minutes or more passed until a man walking his two dogs passed by and answered my plea for help. He tied his dogs to the other gatepost and duly guided me one way then the other until he could free the mirror. It was slightly damaged, but only the small reflector bulb had become dislodged. I thanked him and he went on his way, while I found the key to the property and unpacked the car. This incident made me acutely aware of how vulnerable I was without any friends or neighbours around. I would just have to rely on God then!

Over the next ten weeks I disciplined myself to write this book. Each morning after an early-morning walk and breakfast, I sat at the dining table, looking out onto the view – a field, cottages, more fields and the sea, with Coquet Island just to the right. On a clear day, from the front two bedroom windows Warkworth Castle could be seen, with its very distinctive keep. This was my writing environment. I set myself a deadline; the first draft was to be completed by Christmas. I would aim to include additional walks and a final chapter by mid-January, my leaving date.

Alternate afternoons were spent on the beach at Alnmouth and Mirk loved it. Initially, off the lead, he would run to greet other dogs and their owners and always waited until I caught up with him, or returned to me. He got to know the people with treats in their pockets, and would sit very patiently at their feet, looking up at them until he was rewarded.

On one such afternoon we met Pete with his three terriers. They lived in a converted barn and he was having trouble with his central heating. On another occasion we met a lady who always had treats in her pocket, walking along with her black spaniel. There was also a Scottish lady from Melrose who was looking after her sister's dog whilst she was recovering from an operation. And then there was Dianne, who I first met in 'Caboose', a delightful patisserie in Warkworth, where she worked. One day, she was serving and I thought that her hair looked lovely and dared to tell her so. She replied that her hairdresser was a lady called Emma who worked in the spa at Longhoughton. *A spa?* I thought, *that might be nice; perhaps I could find time for a swim or a facial too?*

Driving along through Longhoughton a few days later, I passed a Spar shop on the right, and the post office on the left, before continuing out of the village. I hadn't seen anything that looked like a hotel or a spa. I managed to do a neat three-point turn in the entrance to a field without hitting the gate and retraced my route back through Longhoughton. As I needed some milk anyway, I stopped at the post office – where else would I go for milk! Inside, I enquired about the whereabouts of the hairdressers.

"In the spa," she said.

"The spa? But I didn't see any hotel complex," I replied.

She smiled, as if she'd explained this many times. "No, the Spar shop," she said. "The hairdressers is in the shop."

I thanked her, went over to the Spar and promptly booked an appointment. How quaint! A hair salon in a grocery shop – whatever next? But why not?

***

Mirk and I also met Dianne's friend Zoe, with her puppy Mia, who was very excitable and never still. Walking around the estuary was a good short walk if the wind was too bracing on the beach. This changed, depending on the tide. When the tide was out, herons and curlew could be spotted. The curlew, redshank and smaller birds would use their different-sized beaks to find food in the mudflats.

About nine weeks into our Northumberland visit, while down on the beach, near the mouth of the estuary, Mirk heard a gun being fired and at this he raced off into the high dunes. I called him and followed as quickly as I could. After several minutes he reappeared around the side of the sand dunes and just sat there! I put his lead back on and tried to continue along the beach, but Mirk was having none of it. At every opportunity, he crouched into the sand dunes and wouldn't budge. Having to coax him out, with lots of rewards both verbal and non-verbal, meant that a usual 45-minute walk took over an hour. This behaviour lasted for the remainder of our stay, which meant that his previous freedom of the beach had become considerably restricted. Clearly this had spooked Mirk quite badly. Sometimes, he took ages to even get out of the car, and then he would just pull me towards the 'Dandelion'. This was a great place for refreshments including ice creams. Part of a Holiday Fellowship Hotel, there was a conservatory area with wicker furniture and seating outside. The waitress would even put a glass of water on the order for Mirk, as he always went to the bowl first. This was our refuge: any friends that visited, Maureen and Richard, Stella and Ian, Dawn, Louise and Tim, Emily, and Joyce all became familiar with the place.

***

Christmas was spent with my friend Yvonne down at her daughter, Amanda's home in North Shields while Amanda and her partner Neil visited his mother and family in Buckingham. Yvonne was looking after their dog, Bob, a Border terrier, whom Mirk had met many times before. We went to Tynemouth Beach on Boxing Day, as did everyone else, it seemed! Again, Mirk was ill at ease. As we were walking back parallel to the road, a lady stopped Mirk to give him some attention. As she walked towards him she could see that he was not happy. I explained Mirk's behaviour on the beach to her, and she shared the story of her own dog, now departed. Mirk always responded positively to people's kindness, but then don't we all. A smile or a few kind words make all the difference, to people and pets alike. Bob, too, despite losing his eyesight, would warm to people taking the time to talk to him. He seemed to like Mirk and showed his affection by standing in front of him, placing his two front paws either side of his face, and licking him. Mirk was very tolerant as usual, allowing Bob to do this, turning his face first one way then the other.

***

Returning to Shilbottle seemed bleak with all the festivities over. I looked forward to Emily's third visit in a few days' time. Another visit to Warkworth was in order, especially as, since Mirk's newly acquired 'allergy' to beaches, we spent alternate days here doing a short, circular walk, half of which was along the river footpath. Mirk loved this, as he was unleashed once we had passed the parked cars alongside the River Coquet. Even here though, on hearing a gun fired, he would take off and I would follow in haste, calling for him to stop, which he always did eventually, and our walk would continue. I liked this stretch of the river; there were two pairs of goosanders, herons, a cormorant, numerous mallards, and on one occasion, an otter! It was along this river, nearer to the bridge, that I saw my first kingfisher very many years ago; but you never forget your 'firsts', do you?

Some days, especially Fridays which were our 'days off', we ventured further afield. Cragside (National Trust) was a favourite as it was possible to eat outside in the courtyard or on the picnic tables and benches around the front. The food here was great; a good variety of hot meals and snacks.

There were numerous well-signposted walks, with helpful accompanying leaflets. On one occasion finding Cragside closed just before Christmas, we continued on to Rothbury where we found 'Tomlinsons'. This is a great place which caters for cyclists, walkers and their dogs! Again, the food and coffee were great. It is located on the corner of Bridge Street and was the old school house. Cutting off by the side of the graveyard opposite the church are some steep steps, which lead down to the riverside. There are good walks on either side, where the path runs alongside the river. These routes are a good way to walk off lunch or create an appetite for tea for both you and your dogs.

***

I made the best of being separated from my new home in Cockermouth. I dared not even think about it before my departure as, I now believe, I would not have left. The idea to write was the good bit and my routine became excessively entrenched – doing similar things each and every day, even down to the food I ate. Mirk, of course, was used to a routine and being fed the same food, so he got to know what time it was by our activities. (For a few years before my retirement, I dispensed with my watch and learned to know the time by listening to my body.) Getting up when I woke up, eating when I was hungry, and sleeping when I was tired suited me. Even though I had a clock in the kitchen and in the car, and a mobile, I did not want to become a slave to time. Provided that I kept all my appointments, and had a strict diary regime, then I was fine. Mirk was the same. He couldn't tell the time any other way than by listening to what his body was telling him. Every day, without fail, he knew when it was his mealtime. At around 5pm, he would sidle up to the settee or where I was sitting, and press his head against my leg. When my affection stopped, he would push his nose under my hand for me to continue. This would go on until I got up to feed him. Once he had had his supper, he would then settle down to sleep until his last visit outside, just prior to bedtime.

After Christmas, and with Emily's final visit over, there seemed little else to keep me from returning, and with the bulk of the book written, I decided to leave a week earlier than scheduled. We left Shilbottle but spent a few days away in Battlesteads, before returning to Cockermouth on 12 January 2012. Battlesteads was a bit of a luxury for us, especially the food which I ate in the bar with Mirk at my feet. This was very much a dog-friendly pub, even supplying poo bags, green towels and doggy treats, all as part of their room service.

Staying in Durham for a few days en route home, walking in Houghall Woods delighted us both. We walked happily on paths around the agricultural college, where the remains of a settlement, a long-deserted village, can still be seen along the Houghall Trail. It was built to serve the pit which was worked only briefly during the 1840s. A century later, three streets which were still standing were taken over by the National Coal Board until 1955 when these too were demolished. The only visible remains are the concrete bases of the houses, a row of front door steps and further along, a circular enclosure where the pit shaft would have been. Many bricks remain strewn about – with LOVE inscribed on them. These were manufactured at the brick foundry of the mine owner, Joseph Love.

> 'They shut the road through the woods,
> Seventy years ago;
> Weather and rain have undone it again
> And now you would never know
> There was once a road through the woods
> Before they planted the trees'
>
> Kipling *The Way Through The Woods*

After four days, the car was again packed with our belongings. We gave a fond farewell to our host, Kirsty, and we were once again on our way, taking the slip road at Scotch Corner, and then right to the A66. The day was bright and crisp, and very soon we were passing Penrith, then on to Keswick. Here, we stopped for a while. Mirk enjoys his freedom on Fitz Park, and with two-hour parking along the road by the youth hostel, we had plenty of time to enjoy it. Latrigg was still there, a fell we had climbed over a year ago with a National Park ranger. We sauntered through the town, making sure that all was as it was when we had left.

We continued along to Cockermouth, taking the Embleton Road which runs parallel to the A66, and came into the town via Castlegate Drive. We turned left into the Market Place, then right into Kirkgate, parked on the cobbles and then knew that we were home. When I opened the boot, Mirk stood, sniffing the cold air, and then, on recognising his surroundings, jumped from the car and headed across the road to No 26. Home at last – what a relief!

Mirk's Favourite Walks

KESWICK (1) – Derwent Water

There are many possible walks from here but these are just two that Mirk particularly enjoys. From the boat hire landing stages trips around Derwent Water can be made, and as well as great views, a return or single ticket will allow you to get off and on again at any of the landing stages to walk back to Keswick. We like to alight at High Brandlehow, close to the southern end of the water. Turning right to walk along the path can be a leisurely stroll with ample time to watch the activity on the water – be it birdlife or children playing! After passing Hawes End, the path goes slightly inland, through Fawe Park – where Beatrix Potter spent some time on holiday – to the boathouse at Nicol End. Here, amongst all the sailing enthusiasts, can be found a café with outside tables overlooking the landing stage.

Continuing on, picking up the road into Portinscale, past the hotel and Derwent Hill, the path turns right, crossing Stormwater Bridge. A path now turns right, running between fields and leading back into Keswick at the road by the bridge opposite the entrance to the Pencil Museum. There's a place to sit inside with Mirk called Temporary Measure, where not only will you find a "lovely cup of tea" but also artwork by Emma, and lots of lovely knitted items by her mum. A single knitted rabbit has expanded into a range of story books, ceramic mugs, bowls and babywear. Your photographs can be turned into canvases or prints and a quote added – either one of your own or provided by Emma. This is a lovely place to linger and return to. Once refreshed, you can continue along the road into the town.

Keswick's Theatre by the Lake is wonderful and in the evenings after Mirk has been fed, he just falls asleep, so it is often an ideal time to visit. On one such occasion, I went to see Noel Coward's *Hay Fever*. During the interval, I took my non-alcoholic drink to the entrance of the foyer for some fresh air. I was followed by a man who enquired, "Is it raining again?" "Does it matter?" I replied. "No, I suppose not," he replied. How sad, I thought, that the topic of the rain should be at the forefront of the conversation. So I said, "Here we are, in a great little theatre, with Derwent Water just metres away, surrounded by magnificent fells – albeit shrouded in mist – with three Herdwick sheep sheltering under a tree less than three metres away. Where else could this be? It is just the best place on earth to be, and I wouldn't be anywhere else." He looked shocked, and then hastily retreated inside to finish his ice cream. So, let it rain, hail, snow – I'll still be here.

Keswick (2) – View from Castlehead Wood – Castlehead View

Not all walks need to take all day; in fact one of the best walks in Keswick is one which requires minimum effort for maximum views.

It was in April 2011 that we did such a walk with friends – the Huitsons from Bath – who were on holiday and staying at Greta Hall. This is the former home of several of the Lakeland Poets including Samuel Taylor Coleridge and Robert Southey. Other literary visitors include William and Dorothy Wordsworth, Lord Byron, Keats, Shelley, Sir Walter Scott, De Quincey and Ruskin. Nowadays, it offers quality self-catering accommodation.

Mirk and I, together with Louise, met up with the Huitsons and they introduced us to this excellent walk.

From the town centre, passing the Tourist Information Centre, walk up St Johns Street and continue along onto Ambleside Road, before turning right along Springs Road. A short distance along on the right is a footpath. Take this right turn along a narrow lane to the end, until you reach Castlehead Wood. Ascend the path to the right through the wood. After a short while, there is a rocky section which will bring you to the top of Castlehead View. There are wooden benches here, and as a picnic had been provided by Joyce, we sat and admired our surroundings. Mirk also had his lunch, water and a dental stick. He was now back on his lead to prevent him wandering off. Over Derwentwater, to the right, was Swinside, with Catbells to the left. An interpretation board marks out all the other fells, so it is well worth the effort, especially on a fine day.

Leaving the top, we head downwards to meet a path that forks left or right. Either route eventually meets the B5289. Cross the road, to find a path into Cockshot Wood, then turn right which will lead you to the Theatre by the Lake. Continue along, walking through Hope Park – dogs on leads – and back into the centre of Keswick. The café by the bicycle shop, The Pedlar, has tables outside and a water bowl for dogs. Excellent food is served here though it is often busy. In the Market Square there are many other cafés with outside tables.

Crummock Water
OS OL4 North-Eastern area

When Mirk and I are in the caravan during the summer months it is not necessary to go very far afield to find new and interesting walks. Turning right along the B5289 towards Lorton, past the Hundith Hill Hotel, keep right where the road splits, past Scale Hill holiday cottages and turn left just before Scale Hill Bridge to park in a National Trust car park. This is free to members, but expensive for non-members. It is very small, so is best avoided during the busy times – or alternatively, go early!

Go through a gate which brings you into Lanthwaite Wood. Here there are several paths: the lower one brings you directly to the head of Crummock Water and the views are so beautiful, it's well worth taking a rest here to admire them. Mirk loved to go into the water to cool off and invariably, there would be other dogs to meet and play with. From here, there are paths on either side; the right taking you around the side of the water, which Mirk and I tend to go just a short way round as there are often sheep grazing and therefore he is kept on his lead. Taking the left-hand path eventually leads to a wall where you can then turn left to walk a short distance before it brings you to a road. This is the B5289. Mirk and I usually return by the same route, pausing for a rest on a seat by the boathouse.

Should you take the higher path just after leaving the car park, this climbs steadily upwards to a gate. Go through this gate, which takes you onto a path between fields. This pathway meets the B5299. Turn right, onto the road, and walk past Lanthwaite Gate Farm, over a cattle grid to Lanthwaite Green Farm. Turn right, taking the path through the farm and then on between fields of sheep. On the left at the top of the field, there is a gate straight ahead. Ignore the gate and turn left to walk along the edge of a field by the wall. At the other end of this field is a wooden gate leading back to Lanthwaite Wood. Follow this path round and eventually Crummock Water will come into view on the left. This path leads down to meet the original path from the car park. To admire the views at Crummock Water, turn left, or turn right back to head back to the car park.

If you are then heading back towards Cockermouth, stop on the way at Newhouse Farm for a cream tea. Picnic tables are at the front, so it is dog-friendly and car parking is round the back of the building.

Whinlatter Forest Park
OS OL4 North-Western area

Perhaps one of Mirk's most favourite walks would be the 'red route' in the forest. Probably because once we have passed the adventure playground, he can be off the lead and free to roam where he pleases. As he knows this route so well, he is often well ahead of me. There are so many different smells and scents from the woodland inhabitants that he is often 'lost' in his own world. He knows where he can find water, not only to drink, but also in which to cool off. He waits at the junctions for me to catch up, and you will not need poo bags – but do make sure your dog poos in the undergrowth not on the footpath. If you need to see why, call in to the toilets for an explanation!

There are so many routes to choose from that it's a good idea to obtain the forest map from the shop, where the staff are really helpful and are always happy to advise. Many hours can be spent here: there is so much to do. With mountain bikes to be hired, and a short zip wire, families will be entertained for hours. And, of course, a visit to the Siskin Café is a must. After freshly prepared food and drinks you may feel the need to do yet another walk and return for tea! Try the 'blue route'. From April to the end of August, the visiting ospreys that have been returning to Bassenthwaite Lake to breed since 2001, can be seen on the CCTV at the visitors centre. These are fantastic birds of prey and many hours can be spent learning about and watching the progress of their offspring until their flight to West Africa in late August.

Across the road from the visitor centre and car park are a number of walks from a little lower down, Revelin Moss being one of them. If you think you may become a frequent visitor, think about getting a 'Discovery Pass' which is a great way to help the Forestry Commission while allowing you to park free for a year. Plus you won't need to worry about change!

Binsey and Uldale
OS OL4 North-Western area

This is a short walk but with magnificent views, both on the drive to it and the walk up it. From Cockermouth take the B5291 towards Bassenthwaite Lake and cross the bridge at the head of the lake. Continue to meet the A591 Carlisle-Keswick road. Turn right at the Castle Inn Hotel, then immediately left to Uldale. Binsey is situated on the left-hand side and can be seen quite clearly on the approach. It is relatively small, 447 metres and rounded. Take a left-hand turn towards Ireby and after a very short distance, turn left again to park along the roadside. Here you'll see a gate on the right, and the path is straight ahead. A steady uphill wander soon brings you to the summit with good views over to the Uldale Fells, across the Solway Firth to Dumfries and Galloway and over to Keswick and Derwent Water, as well as nearer places such as Overwater. After a rest, you can return by the same route. This is a very popular walk particularly at weekends for families.

By now, it could well be lunchtime (or teatime), so go back to the road junction, turn left and continue along to Uldale. At the crossroads, turn right – there is a sign here for Mae's Gallery and Teashop. This was once the village school. With off-road parking, and dog-friendly space, you will receive a very warm welcome, from Mark the owner, along with delicious, freshly baked teacakes and scones. There's also the chance to browse the artwork on the various walls. Sunday lunches here are very popular, and the vegetarian food is excellent.

By now, you are almost at Caldbeck, so having gone back to the main road, turn right to continue over a cattle grid onto Uldale Common and continue into the village of Caldbeck.

The Howk – Caldbeck – about 40 mins

Park in the free car park – Lake District National Parks – in the centre of the village. Leave the car park by the exit route and in a few yards, you will find yourself at the Village Common. Here, there are sometimes sheep, as well as a duck pond, which is situated in old clay dubs.

Turn left and walk a few yards to a house facing a sign on the left-hand wall – 'Public Footpath to The Howk'. Go through the gate and proceed to a further gate. Continue along the path until The Howk is reached. This is a limestone gorge with beautiful waterfalls, and the picturesque ruins of the bobbin mill, together with an interpretation board, can be viewed and enjoyed. Continue along the path, up the steps, passing a bridge over the river, where a few yards further on are some waterfalls, which are worth seeing. Return to the bridge, cross it, and head up the steep steps, making sure to pause on the bridge to look down into the gorge. At the top of the steps, turn left and follow the path along the edge of a field to reach a gate on the roadside. Turn left, following the road back into the village, turning left again to reach the car park on the left, just past the bridge.

For a longer walk, on reaching the road from the field, cross over and turn right along the road by the school. Go over a small bridge across a beck, then fork left, leaving the road. A short distance on, there is a gate on the left. Go through this, across the field – sometimes there are cows in the field – to a gate. Go through the gate, and along a wooded path to come out by some cottages. Continue along the side of the road until you reach the left turn. Turn left here and continue to the car park.

The village is named after the Cald Beck on which it stands. This river, with its tributaries, provided the water for the important industrial development of the area in the seventeenth and eighteenth centuries – woollen mills, bobbin mills, corn mills, a paper mill and a brewery. The village still reflects this industrial activity with many of the old mill buildings still in use.

In Caldbeck there are a variety of lovely eating places. My favourite is at The Priest's Mill. Dogs are welcome outside and water is provided. Car parking is limited here, but can be easily reached from the Lake District NP car park. There are two footpaths, one on either side of the bridge opposite the car park. It is about a quarter of a mile and very pleasant either way. Here you might like to look round the church and graveyard where John Peel the huntsman is buried, but this is not, unfortunately, dog friendly.

Whilst at The Priest's Mill do visit The Wool Clip, a co-operative run by fifteen or so women who spin, dye, knit and crochet, and who have a wealth of knowledge on anything to do with sheep and wool. Having discovered The Wool Clip thanks to my daughter, Louise, who knew of its existence many years ago, I started out by buying a couple of kits, which led on to my designing and knitting mitts, bags and throws. It is not for profit, but to help support the Cumbrian farmers.

Grasmere

When approaching Grasmere from Keswick on the A591, ignore the turning right into Grasmere (B5287) and continue along to a large lay-by on the left-hand side. (If this is full, then continue to a small roundabout, turn right into the village where there is a large car park on the right.)

From the lay-by, carefully cross the road, and you will see a footpath sign by the side of a field leading to Grasmere Village. There are often Herdwick sheep in the field which are my favourite breed of sheep. Their lambs are a delight to watch in the spring. Continue to the end and ahead is a bridge over the River Rothay. Take this to the end where you'll come to the Memorial Garden and church on the left and Wordsworth Hotel on the right.

This is a good place to take refreshments, either entering right to sit outside on the terrace, or continue to the bar just past the main entrance. You can see the world go by seated at the outside tables, or if you prefer the inside comfort, dogs are allowed in the bar. The staff are extremely helpful and courteous and will supply water for both you and your dog.

From the hotel, continue right passing 'The Herdy Shop' which sells items based on the Herdwick sheep and is well worth a visit. Then you will come to the square opposite The Heaton Cooper Gallery. Cross the road, walking left to a lane a few yards along. Turn right into and up the lane, over a cattle grid, (there is a small gate on the left as an alternative, should you and/or your dog not like cattle grids) and continue upwards. On reaching a house on the left, Allan Bank (NT) which is now open to the public, is well worth a visit. Children, dogs and adults are all welcome to share their views on how the building should be used. Mirk has been several times and on our last visit had his photograph taken for their Facebook page.

From here, return to the path and turn left at the footpath sign and continue along this path for a while. Don't forget to look back for good views over towards Helm Crag ahead and Heron Pike to the right. Continue past a house to a gate on the right. Proceed with dogs on leads as there are usually sheep in this field. Head to the bottom of the field where there is another gate, and go through this, to meet the river. There are stepping stones here and the river is shallow so it should be easy to cross. There are sometimes cattle in the field across the river – large beasts who are often standing in the river or on the banks. Head up and across the field to a house on the left and through the gate. Continue past some really nice holiday cottages to reach Easedale Road and turn right over Goody Bridge. Instead of road walking, take the path through the gate on your right, which runs parallel to the road. There are houses on the left-hand side of the road, and before these end, go through a gate on the left to continue along the road for a short distance. By the last house, there is a large gate leading into a wooded area, with Easedale Beck on your left. At the end of the wood, through the gate, turn left and cross the road.

Take a footpath on the right – through the grounds of a hotel -- and follow this round and along till it ends at the A591. Walking right along this road for a very short distance, turn right again and follow this path across a couple of fields to join the pathway into the village. It is time now to take tea in the numerous cafés, many with outside seating. Visit the church and graveyard where many members of the Wordsworth family are buried; or call in the famous Gingerbread Shop; or simply enjoy strolling around the Memorial Garden where the path is made up of slate memorials, some donated by famous people who love the area, or ordinary people like myself (look out for Pete and Jean Maddison, Darlington).

St Oswald's Parish Church is well worth a visit when in Grasmere. According to the plaque near the entrance to the churchyard it is dedicated to "Oswald of Northumbria, King of Christianity" who, it is believed, preached on this site sometime before AD 642, when he died in battle.

It is a Grade 1 listed building of national historic interest. The oldest part dates from around AD 1300, although it is probably the third church to have stood on this ancient site by the side of the River Rothay.

(*OS Explorer DL7 The English Lakes, South Eastern Area*)

Acorn Bank Garden and Water Mill
Temple Sowerby, Penrith, Cumbria

This is another great NT place to visit en route to or from the Lakes as the A66 by-passes Temple Sowerby. It is located only a mile from the A66. I have spent many happy hours here with Mirk on our own or meeting up with family and friends.

There is a herb garden and orchard but dogs are not allowed here. The best walk is along the woodland path down to the Water Mill which is working most weekend afternoons. The Crowdundle Beck winds its way along through the wood where red squirrels live and in the beck itself, otters. Mirk often enjoys this walk twice – in opposite directions, before and after lunch!

In the courtyard there are picnic tables where I always sit, as it is dog friendly. Both the food and staff are excellent, as is the service. The fruit and herbs from the garden are used in the preparation of the food, and you will need to return several times before you have worked your way through the cake and dessert menu!

As this is a National Trust property, there are admission fees, unless, of course, you are a member or you join on the day. If you are staying for any length of time in the Lakes, it may be worthwhile joining if only for the free parking in the many National Trust car parks in the area.

Cockermouth – Harris Park & Cemetery

It was during our stay in a friends' cottage in Kirkgate during the November 2009 floods that we discovered Harris Park. This can be accessed from various locations close to the town, as well as in different directions.

From Kirkgate, turn into Cocker Lane to follow the slope down to a bridge and cross the River Cocker. Note the tiny cottage by the bridge. Cross the bridge and turn left to follow the road into the park. Under a bridge – Lorton Road above you – continue along, ignoring the steps on the right-hand side (just past a lane) which lead onto the bridge that you are about to go under. Stop here, just before going under the bridge. If it is the right time of year and the water shallow, salmon can be seen.

Continue along this path and keep a look out for herons as they can often be seen along the river – standing on stones or flying low. Early morning, dippers are regularly spotted, usually in pairs. These are short-tailed songbirds related to the wren family, and enjoy fast-flowing water where they can swim, dive and even walk under water to feed.

Carry on, passing Rubbybanks Cottage where the path turns right and pass between the cottage and the cottage garden. Go through the kissing gate at the top and turn left to either pick up the river path to the left or stay on the path straight ahead. Both lead to the same point. At the end of the path, turn left over the bridge, pausing to look right upstream with the YHA on the right. Over the bridge turn left. (On the right is a short path, then a kissing gate leading into a field – this is where Mirk found a flock of sheep to herd.) Proceed along the path, with the river now on the left, passing some swings until the path goes into a wooded area. Continue along, until the path meets another.

To the left is the Railway Viaduct over the river and the one which you walked under earlier. Here, there are choices, but for the purpose of this walk, turn right which is now a cycle path and part of the Greenway. Continue along, under a bridge (Lorton Road) and forward. Eventually, you'll come alongside the cemetery, but continue ahead, following the path around the right-hand bend, and through a wrought-iron gate into the cemetery. Dogs on leads here. Various paths lead through the cemetery so it is worthwhile taking your time to read some ancient headstones, and to linger on a seat to spot the red squirrels. They are abundant here, so it is worth a brief pause to enjoy them.

Continuing along, the track runs parallel to the earlier pathway– through a tiny wrought-iron gate on the right to join the path. Turn left. Continue straight on, back the way you came, but this time cross the railway viaduct, taking the steps down on the right to meet up with the earlier path. At the bottom, turn left to walk back along the path/road leading to the town. Look out for the kingfisher along here, spotted on two consecutive days over Christmas 2010.

There are many excellent dog friendly coffee shops and restaurants where you can either take your dog inside or sit outside.

Among the many to choose from there are Tea And Tranquillity in the Market Place, The Coffee Kitchen with the downstairs area open to dogs in Challoner Street and the New Bookshop outside in summer, on Main Street. On Station Road is Veeva on the corner of Mitchell's Auction Rooms. All are highly recommended for their friendliness, good food and coffee, and for supplying water for your dog.

Dodd Wood, Dodd Fell, Mirehouse Gardens

The walk to Dodd Fell through Dodd Wood is already described in the earlier *Move To Cockermouth* chapter, but after taking some refreshments at the Sawmill Tearoom, if you feel like a stroll to the lake, then purchase a ticket at the café for Mirehouse 'grounds only'.

Cross the A591 and show your ticket at the cottage window on the left. While dogs need to be kept on leads, exploring the paths down towards the lake is still worthwhile. Leaving the gardens, go through a gate and across the field of sheep to visit the church of St Bega. Apparently, it was this tiny church which Tennyson had in mind when he described St Bedevere carrying the dead King Arthur in his poem *Morte d'Arthur*;

> "... to a chapel in the fields
> A broken chancel with a broken cross,
> That stood on a dark strait of barren land ..."

Go back across the field, bearing to the right towards a gate. Go through the gate, to find the path which is easy to follow down to the water's edge. Spend some time sitting by the lake, because between April and August you just may see an osprey flying low over the water looking for fish. These are spectacular birds of prey, and have returned to breed in this area since 2001.

The path turns left back towards the house; it is easy to follow and one really cannot get lost. Another stroll through the grounds brings you back to the road and the car park opposite.

Warkworth, Northumberland – Circular by the Castle and River Coquet

This is a lovely walk any time of year. Out of season, there is ample parking in Dial Place or just further along the road by the church, towards the river, there are more parking places.

Follow the path along the river on your right. Dogs are fine off the lead here right along to the end. Pass through a kissing gate into a field, at the end of which is the English Heritage Hermitage (in season, a boat will take you across to the opposite side to see this). Dogs on lead here. At this point turn left to walk up a tarmac road past Howlett Hall heading uphill. As the road levels out, look for a signpost on the left. Turn left here walking along the edge of a field, with houses on the right. Ahead is a good view of Warkworth Castle.

Following the pathway round, go through an obvious gate, and across another field to join the path by the castle. This is well worth a visit. The ruins are significant, and dogs are allowed into the grounds and ruins on leads. A free audio tour guide gives the history of the Percy family, whose lion emblem can be seen carved throughout parts of the castle. (Should you park here, your car-parking fee is deducted from the admission price.)

Continue along the pathway, down some steps and then the path continues into the village, by Castlegate House. Walk downhill and back to Dial Place.

While there may be some pubs which allow dogs, I thoroughly recommend that you feed and water your dog, and leave him in the car with windows slightly open, before treating yourself to a visit to 'Cabosse'. This is a delightful boutique and licensed coffee shop established in 2008 by Louise Frederique who creates fine French-style chocolates and continental patisserie. This is so good, it is the only place where I leave Mirk in the car – but not in hot weather – to visit.

Cabosse Limited

5 Dial Place, Walkworth, NE65 0UR

Tel; 01665 712644

www.cabossechocolates.co.uk

Mirk at Crummock Water

About the Author

Jean Tyers was born in Nottingham and spent most of her adult life working as a probation officer in Durham, where she lived with her two daughters.

Retired in 2008, Jean used some of her leisure time working as a conservation volunteer and spent time on working holidays with the National Trust, NTS and the RSPB throughout the UK. Jean moved to Cockermouth two years later with Mirk, her Border collie. Recently, Jean began to teach swimming. She and Mirk enjoy their daily walks.

This is her first book.

About the Illustrator

Kathryn Brame completed a BA (Hons) in Fine Art at Northumbria University in 2007 and has since been exhibiting work throughout the UK and internationally. She is also due to complete a Masters in Fine Art from Newcastle University in 2014. Kathryn's work centres on absence, memory and the fragility of existence by capturing snapshots of the everyday and giving these moments presence through drawing, painting, film and installation.

kathrynbrame.com.